Hush

Hush

A memoir unravelling the unintended
legacy of family secrets

MICHELLE SCHEIBNER

THE
KIND
PRESS

www.thekindpress.com

This book is for my mother,
Esmee Ponsonby Scheibner.

Contents

Part One
Family Secrets

Part Two
Evolving

Part Three
Belonging

A Note from Michelle

Our heritage may be different, your parents of another generation, you may have close family members, but these facts aren't important right now. My hope for you is that *Hush* gives you permission for further self-enquiry. As I take the stories out of my backpack and share them with you, please take time to read past the details. You may have tried many methods to heal pain, find answers and to understand repeating and limiting patterns, yet there is still something in your life that remains out of reach. Something that persists, like a thorn in your finger repeatedly prickling you because you can't remove it.

Although this is my story, it's intended to enrich the conversation you have with yourself about your story. To encourage you to put aside your complaints and private fears and see your life with a new and curious lens. You are more than your current and past story. I wrote this book as a companion to take with you on the path of new discovery, rather than a panacea to fix your problems. Yes, there will be tears and grief, but it is nothing like you how you feel right now. Finding ways to honour a new story, to reconcile and make meaning of heartache may shift the blame and shame to compassion.

Hush encourages you to focus on three pillars of your identity:
Your heart: feelings, emotions the place where your empathy resides.
Your mind: thoughts, behaviours, memories, decisions and choices.
Your body: genetic foundation.

At the centre of these three pillars is your very special magic, that only you possess.

Prologue

As a girl, my favourite place was a corner of the bay window in the 'music' room. We called it the music room because Grandmother's upright piano was against one wall and Dad's treasured radiogram was in the back corner. A soft, sheer lace curtain created a layer that disturbed the clarity of my vision whilst aiding my purpose. Outside that window were enough flowering shrubs and trees for me to remain unseen as I kept watch.

There was always a sofa or armchair in this niche, depending on my mother's current decorating whim. I could easily kneel on the seat, lean my elbows on the back, rest my face in the palms of my hands, and watch. From here, I could see the path all the way to the front gate. If I glanced away for a second and the gate opened, I recognised the click and my attention quickly picked up the visitor.

I was about seven the day when, from my fort, I recognised the dentist walking up the path. Panic.

Mum didn't tell me Mr Watson was coming here! I hate the dentist. Why wouldn't she tell me? Why is he here?

If I crouch lower and duck my head, he won't see me, and I can listen. The doorbell signals his arrival, and my mother is walking swiftly down the hall in response. Maybe he has come to see Auntie Daphne. *Hang on, why am I home from school today? And it's too early for visitors. We haven't had breakfast yet.* Mr Watson follows my mother into the kitchen.

I'm still lost in thought, trying to gather clues when I hear the gate again. Dare I look? Slowly, I raise my head just enough for one eye to do its job. Dr Field!

Why didn't they tell me the doctor was coming today?

Doorbell again, Mum repeats the greeting and again on entry, they head to the kitchen. I hold my breath and carefully slide my feet from under me to the floor so I can edge behind the full-length, steel-blue drape framing the window.

This feels safe and secure. They can't see me. My heart is beating quickly as I strain to listen for clues.

'Michelle.'

I hear my name.

'Michelle?'

They're all talking about me. This can't be good.

What is happening? Why didn't they tell me?

Now Mum is calling me! Why? I can hear her footsteps. She knows where I am! Better to get to my bedroom and close the door. Too late. They're already in the music room, and Mum's hands are around my waist. She has a firm hold and Dr Field is in the room, too, looking at me. I resist and try to run again, but I'm grabbed from behind and carried to the kitchen where the table is now standing in the centre of the room covered with a white sheet. I can hear my own confused crying. I'm so terrified. *What is happening?*

Mr Watson steps up to the table and I can't see Dr Field. Why can't I see Dr Field?

'You hold her shoulders, Mrs Scheibner, I have her legs.'

Now Dr Field has moved to a soothing voice and is saying, 'Shhh, shhh, it's okay. Better for you if you don't struggle!'

And then he's standing over me and adeptly placing a round bowl-shaped thing over my face.

'Take a deep breath,' he repeats, while before my eyes weirdly moving shapes are spinning back into my head.

Why? Why didn't they tell me?

Part One

Family Secrets

"The parents eat sour grapes, and the children's teeth are set on edge."

Ezekiel 18:2 (New International Version)

CHAPTER 1

Ground Zero

I'm not a mother.
I'm not a partner or soul mate.
I'm no longer a daughter.
I'm not a sister.
I'm not a widow or divorced.
I'm not a next of kin.
I'll never be a grandmother.

~

I look at the clock. It's 10.06 am on Tuesday, 26 January 2016. Music is softening the room. God is waiting for this particular track—Adele singing *'Make You Feel My Love'*—to finish before finally hitting stop on Chris's life. He admired this song, basking in the tone and depth of her voice. Together and separately, we'd made our own meaning of the lyrics. None of that mattered now.

There's a particular silence in the moment as you wait for another breath. I'm holding mine, Chris wrapped in my arms. I watch, searching for the next rise of his body, and finally he is still. There is no next breath. The music has softened the room, and now there is no sound. No longer any laboured breathing. For the first time in my life, I'm experiencing being in the presence of another human being as their soul departs their physical body. Chris was a believer in the old-style analogue alarm clock. One sits on the shelf next to the bed and continues to tick, tick, tick as if this is a regular day.

It's not a regular day. Yes, the sun is shining in from the garden, working its way between each leaf, pushing its way into the room to witness the final event. There is nothing regular about this. Chris is My Person! My constant companion. The one human who knows as much of my story as I do. There is no label for who I am now.

Five minutes ago, I was his carer, his Enduring Power of Attorney, the first point of contact, the person he trusted with his life. There is no life to tend now. I'm just 'the friend'. I have been the other set of ears at all his medical appointments. I have sat in the café with my best girlfriend, Bec, as we waited out the hours while his surgery was performed. I am the person the surgeon called to say the operation was successfully over. Now I'm just 'the friend'.

Friend. This one word cannot possibly convey the depth and complexity of the dynamic between Chris and me. As the 'friend', my grief doesn't have an acceptable place to fit. Had I still been his partner, de facto, lover, my grief would be recognised, expected, accepted, listened to. How will I explain to people what life will be like for me now?

My heart has been fraying for weeks and all I want is to lie here with him in a private moment of honour and peace. But I can't. His number two daughter is here.

'I'll leave you to have a moment with your dad,' I say and regretfully leave them. The spell is broken. This is it.

Heading to the kitchen, I'm resetting my head. Yesterday, the doctor gave me a To Do list in anticipation of this moment. With each pace down the hallway, I'm stepping back into my mantle of capable, organised, reliable, professional Michelle.

Of course, you've got this!

CHAPTER 2

First Step

It's late 2016 and I'm driving down Hotham Street, ten minutes away from The Grove. I like coming this way. It's familiar, only a short distance from where I grew up, and takes me through the heart of a community where Jewish families feel safe and supported in their belonging. I've always been curious about the lives of others. I wonder what it's like to live in a tight community. I don't fit with any 'community'.

I'd tried an Anglican community again a couple of years ago and it didn't go well. At the first service I went to, there was a 'greeter' to welcome new faces. I arrived solo, and her greeting method was to ask a lot of questions that I hadn't expected and wasn't ready for. Are you married? No. Divorced? No. Do you have children? No. She didn't quite know what to do with me and I didn't know how to find my place within the family-centric community. I persisted and joined the small, group bible study program, but they were all couples and most had children, so it wasn't long before I stopped forcing myself to go.

Now, I notice I've entered the enclave of an Orthodox Jewish community. I'm fascinated. I begin playing a game with myself about how much I notice.

The traffic is heavy, so I can take my time with my observations as I sit in the queue of cars. There is a busyness about the many pedestrians walking with speed and intention. The majority are men. Some have the hand of a son; others are pairs or groups of tweenage boys. The starkness of their black suits stands out against the warmth of the spring day. Spring is signalled from the gardens where I can 'see' the scent of Jasmine and its light feminine sway. It serves to make the black suits look blacker and the masculine dominance of the foot traffic all the more obvious—all walking in the one direction, toward the meeting place of the synagogue I presume—all striding with purpose and intention despite the heat.

My fascination moves to curiosity. Why black suiting even on such young boys? I recognise the yarmulkes on the youngers and wonder at the significance of the large black hats on the elders that look like they should be in a New York streetscape. All ages wear the payot, or side curls, along with the tallit (prayer shawl).

The traffic has picked up the pace and I redirect my focus back to the vehicle in front. All the time, my mind continues to wonder about the time of day and the rules so visibly displayed in those characters, like large ants, scampering in the one united direction. I'm pulled back from my mindful wanderings by the GPS announcing, 'Turn left now and then immediately left again. Your destination is on the left.'

It's a residential street lined with cars, and parking is limited. I manage to find a space and am pleased to notice I still have ten minutes before the scheduled time. I take the opportunity to regroup my thoughts and wonder for the hundredth time if this will be worth the fifty-minute drive. It needs to be. I desperately need to get back to some sense of normality, and I so hoped Katrina was right about Sarah.

CHAPTER 3

Breaking Point

It had been a day in October 2016, and as was my habit, I took a seat by my office window to make the call to Katrina, a client I had both coached and provided services to for over a decade. The elevated aspect offered me a safe view from the privacy of my haven, through the heavy branches of the Grandiflora Magnolia, out into the world. Seeing the world from behind the safety of glass has been a constant.

There are so many anchors to grief. Remembering in the moment before making the call how Chris's same tree varietal at his house had dwarfed the For Sale sign with its SOLD sticker, the final salute to the world of his passing. It was a defiant resistance to the closure of a chapter, as if repaying Chris for the years of care and nurturing he'd provided it.

The client call did not go well, and my response really shocked me. Rapport with my clients had always been professional, understanding and accommodating, even in the face of rejection. But on this day, for the first time in twenty years, rather than ask for clarification, I challenged their decision not to go ahead with the project. I had submitted the proposal as I'd inched my way back to the world of work and away from the grief of losing Chris.

The dam burst. I wanted to say, *Don't you understand that just bringing myself through my past into the present has been exhausting? Doing it on my own has been draining. My mind constantly sits on the edge of a cliff, wanting to spill over. Behind my eyes is the source of an endless waterfall. It's as if the neural pathways in my brain have carved the deepest rivers—all rushing in unison to the same cliff!*

But I didn't say any such thing. Instead, I sounded peeved and complained they had unreasonably moved the goalposts. Katrina quietly asked me if it was time I 'spoke to someone.' Feeling like a rag doll with worn stuffing, I limply requested the details, thanked her, ended the call and burst into tears.

It was nine months on since Chris died. My world was imploding, and my business had stalled. Throughout Chris's treatment, I had managed to keep delivering work as it was requested. Now, my personal private life had finally and overwhelmingly collided with my capacity to effectively manage my professional world.

Previously, I'd been able to push through the uncertainty of retrenchments, the loss of parents, relationship failures. Over time, I had created a carefully crafted public brand that was devoid of personal details. I'd learnt from my first career in secondary teaching not to let the students into my personal and private world. This was reinforced in all the training I had completed as a counsellor and then as an executive coach. The focus was always on the world of the client—not me.

Having worked for three decades in career development and career management, I had worked with every type, from natural leaders to individual contributors, from entrepreneurs to CEOs, from those who have to create to those who must serve. I know every individual has their own internal compass of what success looks like, their own set of values and motivators powering them, and yet I was not applying any of that awareness to myself.

The days, weeks and months from the time of Chris's diagnosis, through his surgery, through the cycles of chemo, through the oncologist announcing that the only next step was palliative care, through to the last weeks, days, moments, breaths, through the funeral, through the time spent tying up his life, through the challenge to the will, through the months of working on his house, and then handing it over to new owners, I kept going.

But when that stopped, and I didn't have a reason to get up and tackle another thing on the list, I found myself bouncing around as if in one of those big jumping castles, from one pocket of grief, sadness and emptiness to another. The familiar but undefined melancholy of my childhood was amplified now. There was a hope-less-ness about the future.

In these various pockets, often after midnight, clues would run riot in my brain. I would think about my father. And then I would think about my mother. And I would bounce again. And what made it all so difficult was that I did not have anyone close to me who could compassionately say to me, 'Tell me more about what it is like to walk in your shoes right now.' I was unable to make any sense of my thoughts and feelings.

I had wonderful friends. But there wasn't anyone who knew all about me, or could help give me a compass reading for what I was experiencing. In the stillness and darkness of the early hours, I would secretly plan to disappear, repeating a thought process I'd commenced in my teenage years. *If I just wandered off to the other side of the world, without notice and trace, I wouldn't be missed, and eventually I would die alone, like I was invisible, unheard, and like I had never existed.*

In that moment, on the phone with Katrina, I was painfully aware I had not landed where my younger self had dreamed I would. Instead, I was stuck in quicksand, and I had no plan for how I would be rescued. Unexpectedly, there I was, without the one person who knew many factors of my life and therefore my identity. And the grief was magnified.

Later in the day, I made the call to Sarah.

CHAPTER 4

Healing Begins

As instructed, when I arrived at The Grove Counselling & Therapy centre, I followed the path from the front gate down the side of the house, dipping under the overgrown Cecile Brunner climbing rose blooms. The garden style served as a date stamp for the house. I was only a few kilometres from my family home and even closer to my old school. Returning to a familiar location added an uncanny element to what I was hoping was about to unfold.

~

The week prior, when I finally phoned Sarah, for the first time in my life I introduced myself as the daughter of a holocaust survivor. It seemed important that I make this clear, yet I had never before applied that label to myself. It was as if instinctively, I knew that the focus needed to come back to me now that the caring for Chris was done, finished, over, and he was gone.

Sarah is a narrative therapist, experienced in working with clients recovering from grief, including those who have been carers for lost loved ones. On our first call, she openly shared her situation with me. Her family of origin is Protestant, and she is married to a man of Jewish faith. On hearing this, my heart knew I had landed safely and made the absolute right call.

We spoke for some time on that first call.

'The best way I can describe what I'm experiencing day after day, sleepless night after sleepless night,' I told her, 'is that losing Chris lifted the top off my brain exposing all the hidden heartache and sorrow for the brother I didn't have. I'm ashamed I didn't ask more questions about him or probe my father more about his upbringing and German culture. I don't remember making a conscious decision not to have children. I feel I'm grieving them, too. And now it feels like I'm heading to the end of my life without a mutually loving partner.'

I paused. There was more …

~

The counselling rooms are in an older-style house, typical of those in this suburb before development arrived. I enter through the back door. Clients are encouraged to make themselves a cup of something from a selection of teas and coffees before ringing the bell and heading into the waiting room. Taking my mug of boiled water, I step around the corner into a peaceful space with soothing music playing, and a scented candle flickers in welcome. Yes, this feels right. I hope meeting Sarah will give me permission to explore the family vault of secrets and give me a way to resolve this repetitive feeling, the empty spaces in my being. I have brought my unrelenting list of complaints about family with me. Unheard and unseen, they've not heard my need to feel their compassion.

Before long, the opening door brings Sarah's beautiful face into my world for the first time. She's tall, confident, with just a hint of quirky. Sarah's room is the front room of the house, facing the gate and street. A cosy couch begs me over and I sit in such a way I can see out the window. Sarah takes the armchair opposite, and her presence is framed by the well-stocked bookshelves on the wall behind her. It is a welcoming and reassuring space.

'Where would you like to start?' Sarah asks.

'The best way I can describe it is that it feels like I've suppressed so much, like I haven't been true, even to myself. I'm used to being on my own, but this feels different. I'm exhausted from trying to find a way to put myself back together.'

'You don't look exhausted! In fact, you look like a fit and strong woman who is very together. Tell me more about the feeling.'

'I had been seeing a grief psychologist, but nothing shifted and after ten visits I gave up,' I continue.

'My nights are still sleepless. I toss and turn until I finally get up and start journalling. The theme of not belonging anywhere or with anyone rolls on through every page. No one understands that even though Chris and I weren't technically in a relationship, we were together,' I say, making talking marks with my hands. 'Even before his diagnosis, our daily thoughts and decisions were worked through together, either on the phone or in a local café over coffee. Chris could always see my perspective when I felt let down or like a low priority within the family dynamic. He was my person.'

Sarah lets me rant and I finally stop talking.

'I can hear the thoughts you've been having. Can you describe for me how you've been feeling?' she asks.

My answer is more of what I'm thinking.

'Where do you feel it in your body? Does it have a colour or a sound?' she prompts me again.

But my thoughts are still in charge, and I recognise I can't get to my feelings. All I can do is wipe away the tears.

~

Recently, my 2.00 am scrawling's had been taking a different direction. The grief, sorrow—no word was comprehensive enough to explain the feeling—ran deep, deep into every internal crevice between organs, tissue, veins and arteries, all wrapped in a melancholy I could not define.

I was here because I needed help.

CHAPTER 5

Empty Spaces

Counselling and therapy weren't new concepts to me. My first encounter had been during university. Toward the end of my first year, my parents suggested I move into residence. I was nineteen years old when they thought I needed to stand on my own two feet. So, off I went, into a small, single room of the Women's Residence, Glenn College La Trobe University. It wasn't long before I was navigating adult relationships and an environment that I didn't quite understand the rules of, without a network to support the transition. Then came the first real break up. I was trying to heal from within an isolated rowboat on the dark, misty lake of a tertiary landscape. It was as if I knew the feeling of lethargy and pain that kept me in bed for five days was greater than simply trying to adjust to a new lifestyle. It was my first attempt at trying to fix the feelings I could not explain, but that instinctively felt like they didn't belong to me.

Alone, with only new acquaintances rather than friends, and an underdeveloped life core, I unfurled internally. This was to become the modus operandi of my adult life. Sleepless until sleep insisted, writing depressing prose between midnight and dawn, ceasing healthy eating and exercise until the waves passed, then re-entering the world sadder than the last time.

This led to my first encounter with counselling. I had seen a poster on the wall at the student union and remembered it also appeared on the list of support numbers near the phone on my floor. Optimistically, I wondered if this could ease the loneliness and confusion I'd been unable to shift.

One session later, I came away with a referral to see the doctor on campus and a script for sleeping pills. I didn't get the pills, nor did I return to the counselling office. I did, however, elect the Counselling specialty when completing my Diploma of Education. A decade later, I undertook a Diploma of Counselling and passed with distinctions. The modality and practice suited me, so when the opportunity presented to undertake post-graduate study in Career Development through the Psychology faculty at Deakin University, I grabbed it. Working full time as a careers counsellor in a secondary school setting, opened the door to ideas around personality profiling, values-based thinking and identity labels acquired through work.

By the time I walked into the rooms in October 2016, I had:
- Spent time with at least three other counsellors over a period of thirty years
- Completed several personal development programs with tag lines like 'Design Your Destiny'
- Travelled to Sydney to do 'The Breakthrough Experience' with Dr John Demartini
- Finished a certificate in Reiki
- Completed another NLP Results Training program
- Taken part in the Landmark Forum
- Studied Astrology
- Joined a meditation group and become a Spiritual Healer
- Read numerous self-help books

By the time I met Sarah that day, I'd lived through:
- The passing of too many years stuck in relationships hoping for the happy-ever-after ending to my story
- Learning that things aren't always what they seem

And I knew grief following:
- The death of my father
- The death of my mother
- The death of the one person who had tried to be so many of those roles for me

All I wanted was to heal the empty spaces created by the absence of assumed titles expected when reaching a certain age of maturity. I never heard a brother Grant call me his 'little sister'. I was never introduced as 'my wife' and no child ever cried 'Mumma' for me. I desperately hoped Sarah would help me resolve the void in my heart.

CHAPTER 6

Genetics

Dear Grant,

It is 1990. I'm in my office at the school where I've taught since I began my teaching career. I'm trying to make myself pick up the phone and make a difficult call.

On my return from England, I moved into the position of full-time careers advisor. The role comes with an office in the library so students can pop in and easily access me and the resources. From my desk, I can look out through a window into the body of the main space, and as it is class time, I can see the library is empty. I'm unlikely to be disturbed.

I close the door. There is a private call I need—no, I want—to make. I've been putting it off, and my stomach is churning. It could be life changing for me and it's connected to you.

This is about you and it's about me and it's about my future. Am I forcing open a chest that should remain locked? Will I be able to bear the answer to the question I have?

Before picking up the phone, I gather my thoughts to form an introduction and purpose statement in my head. I'm thirty-six, recently engaged to be married and believe I still have time to start a family. Yes, this is my first time engaged and although the proposal wasn't the romantic gesture I'd dreamt of, there were cards and gifts and wishes of hope and joy. And despite designing and paying for the ring myself, it somehow validates my place in the world.

First, though, I need to deal with something that has been sitting between my clothes and skin like a secret protective shell for as long as I can remember. I've never articulated it in the form of a conscious statement, but it's a mind shadow. It plays on a loop, repeating the list of babies born into our extended family, who are born with conditions and disabilities, rendering them totally dependent on others to care for their needs during a truncated lifespan.

I'm telling you this because I'd love for you to know and understand the beginnings of your story. In my mind, it began with the information our mum and dad told me about you. The doctors told them your condition was so profoundly impacted by Down Syndrome that you'd require permanent care and wouldn't live past the age of seven. That time has well passed.

I wonder if anyone will ever read this letter read to you?

And then there was Mum's Auntie Daphne, who lived with us in Ponsonby, the family home. She occupied a small room upstairs until her death just before my eighth birthday. When she called for Mum, it sounded like an animal screaming, and I'd run and hide in the tiny room under the stairs, in the dark, breathing in dust. I was scared of Auntie Daphne. I didn't understand what was wrong with her, but she needed Mum's full attention, never joined in family events and so must have been pretty unwell. You're probably wondering why I didn't just ask? Maybe I did. If so, I don't recall her condition being given a name, ever. It was a long time after Daphne died when Mum and Dad finally told me about your condition and gave it a name—Down Syndrome. I unknowingly coupled Daphne and you together in my mind. In the absence of information, I made my own sense of what had been a key feature of my childhood. An uneasy picture was forming.

One day in a perfect world, you'd come and meet Mum's cousin, Helen. She and Mum are very close, and Helen often came and stayed with us. These days, Mum goes to Hobart and stays with Helen. I can't remember the details of this family tree link. I think it's connected to our great-grandmother in some way.

Having Helen in the house lifted the silence. The pattern was always the same. She and Mum would head out together to visit Helen's son, Timmy, who was a permanent resident in Kew Cottages. Details of his condition were never discussed within earshot of me until he passed away at around age fifteen. Or was I fifteen? It's a detail I can't quite pinpoint.

I often wonder if you were still alive then?

And then there's Lisa. A joyous, happy child with a passion for music and Aussie rules football, her idolised team the 'Swannies'. Lisa arrived in this world, the firstborn of our middle cousin Rob and his wife Bev, when I was in senior school. As the youngest in the wider family, I was excited to have a baby arrive. Her development was slow, though, and after many tests the news dropped on us all with a thud. Lisa had profound intellectual and physical complications and was unlikely to develop to a stage of living independently. Mum and Dad said you'd never be able to do that either.

A few weeks ago, with all this weighing in my mind, I went to the GP. If I was going to bring a baby into the world, it was my responsibility to ensure they had the best possible start and could thrive in an unhindered life. Dr Gray began the discussion by warning me that due to my age, time was running out. Then she said, 'You need to get on with it.'

I'd have to do more work to get my future husband across the line now. He had a family—two daughters from a first marriage—and he wanted to give them everything. 'There's no room for another child' was the phrase he used to shut down every mention of babies. My unspoken plan relied on his ego and the temptation to try for a boy baby.

Dr Gray did say that given my mother's history, and my age, there was an additional concern. Her strong advice was to contact the Genetic Clinic set up as part of the Royal Women's Hospital in Parkville. The service helps women like me who may have an increased risk of having a child with a genetic condition by providing a genetic screening test. I left her rooms feeling both encouraged and apprehensive at what such a test might reveal. What are the chances of me having a Down Syndrome baby? They must be pretty high.

I dial the number of the Genetic Clinic. Eventually, I'm put through, and a cheery nurse listens to my pre-prepared and now rushed and garbled introduction. She's used to these emotional inquiries and calmly listens.

'Yes, we can certainly test,' she says, then continues. 'It's not invasive. You organise a blood sample to be taken from your brother and send it to us. Then we'll ask you to come in here to the clinic, and we'll take blood from you and compare. This will tell us if his condition is hereditary or caused by a mistake in cell division during early development of the foetus.'

For a split second, I stop listening. Did she say the screening requires a blood test from you? How's that possible? Hadn't Dad said it was highly likely you wouldn't have lived past age seven?

The voice on the end of the phone is still talking, 'If the result indicates a hereditary link, we can look at further testing to give you as much information as possible so you're making an informed decision.'

I thank her and end the call.

What I anticipated would be a simple question has now become more complex. But I'm buoyed by the sound of possibility in her voice. Surely Mum will see how important this is to me. After all, I'm approaching the age she was when she gave birth to you. Yes, I know she legally gave you up, but she must have stayed in contact with Kew to track your development and life?

I immediately make the second call to Mum before the bell for lunch rings and the library bursts alive again.

Can I share a secret with you, Grant? I've always wanted to name my child after our paternal grandmother, Elly. Dad would say I resemble her, and many agree I'm nothing like our mother to look at. Mum is elegant and always composed. For her era, she is considered tall at five-foot-eight and, like her sister, mother and grandmother, of a solid build. Mum has an hourglass shape with a rounded belly and her weight fluctuates, although she never ventures past a size sixteen. Her eyes are sapphire blue and always look sad. Her skin tans if enough baby oil and brown vinegar are applied. She's the same height as Dad, which is also the height I stopped growing. She's calm and more quietly spoken than her extrovert sister. Mum is an introvert in every way. As a kid, I'd look at her and wonder if she really is my mother, so unlike we look. The family joke was she found me in the cabbage patch with Dad—there was no doubt I was his daughter. I had this thick, dark, chocolate-brown hair, his European olive skin and the same face shape, lips and dark brooding eyes with hooded lids. I wonder if you look like Dad. I bet you do.

I'm dialling Mum's number, weighing up what response I'll get. She and I speak several times a week, about events, people, my work. We rarely speak of feelings, and if we do, it's about my disappointment with friends or work. She never ever speaks to me of her feelings, especially about you. Dad passed away almost fifteen years ago, and she has never expressed her grief to me. She is stoic, upright and reliable as she continues to live in the big family home alone and with a loyal but small group of friends around her.

'Hi there!' I begin in my chirpiest tone and launch straight into small talk. I am not good at difficult conversations, especially with those close to me. There's a history of silence around the topic of you and, despite knowing I'm stepping on delicate ground, I must push forward.

'I've just had a very interesting call with the Genetic Clinic RWH.'

Silence.

'Did you know that they can test for genetic indicators like Down Syndrome?'

Silence.

'I really want to do this.'

Silence.

'I'm getting married, and I need to know before I run out of time to have a baby.'

Silence.

'The nurse says it requires comparing my blood profile to Grant's. Do you think he's still living at Kew?'

When she finally speaks, the tone is cold, matter of fact, clinical really.

'I can't help you. I told you all I knew when you were seventeen. We were advised to give him up into care, and not to have contact with him. Wards of the State most likely have a name change. I don't know.'

Now I'm feeling guilty for even speaking your name as I know it will potentially upset her. I revert to obedient child and end the call. My only option now is to dial a third number.

'Hello, this is Kew Cottages, how can I help you?' the voice says. I explain I'm looking for my brother, Grant Phillip Scheibner, carefully spelling out S C H E I B N E R for the millionth time in my life.

'We don't have a resident by that name. It's likely that he passed away some time ago if he was as profoundly affected as you say, but there is no record of him ever being here.' The voice hangs up.

The oxygen leaves my lungs. I hang up the phone and sit, unable to move. This was supposed to clear the slate and give me space to process what to do, to uncover what I need to know so I can get on with planning the place of a child in my world. Now there are more questions.

Will I press ahead and try to convince my fiancée to change his mind about having children? Or will I take the easy option and hand it over to fate? Or am I just like our mother, who, when asked why she didn't have more children, would say she wasn't really very maternal? Had I adopted this phrase, too, and did I really believe it? How do I know? Didn't I always assume I would have a child when married? Why hadn't I asked Mum sooner? What was wrong with me? Does that mean they were right, and you didn't make your eighth birthday? And does this mean you are now officially missing from our family?

Love, 'Chelle x

CHAPTER 7

Breadcrumbs

It's April 2017. The day is hot and humid, the sun beating through a steady northerly wind that's flicking up dust and memories. Even the beach, usually my soothing place, would be avoided today. The gusty conditions transport me back to the schoolyard of my teaching years and the way the wind never failed to turn Year Nine Humanities students into ratty opponents after lunch break.

I've been faffing around all morning, trying to run out of time so I can put it off until tomorrow. I can't though. I must tackle this task today, and not only because the real estate agent made it clear that decluttering always works in favour of the vendor. Yesterday, Sarah urged me to get into the storage space at the back of the garage in the hope of uncovering documents, letters, anything that can shed light on the family history. She was referring to the load transferred here twenty-four years ago, after Mum's passing.

~

Sarah had asked me how I was feeling about my decision to sell the house in Heidelberg. She knew the emotional wrench I'd faced finalising Chris's house. What she didn't know was I'd packed up a deceased's house once before, the house built by my great-grandmother, Flora Louise Ponsonby Thompson. The house was always referred to simply as 'Ponsonby'. The black and white nameplate over the front gate ensured the neighbourhood knew where she lived. There were vague explanations as to the exact origin of the name—all emanating from New Zealand, Kitty's birthplace.

Flora was a local identity, active in the nearby branch of the Red Cross and one of the most tireless charitable workers in Melbourne. She'd accumulated properties around Windsor, Prahran and Caulfield, and the source of her wealth became part of family folklore. Photos of Flora show a large, dour determined-looking woman. There is no mistaking her resolve to leave a legacy for her daughter Daphne. The complicated will did not state why Daphne needed a guardian. It did name my mother as the person to fulfil that role which granted her life tenancy of Ponsonby as long as she cared for 'Daphne and her affairs'. It concluded that upon my mother's death, the dwelling known as 'Ponsonby' will be sold and the 'entire proceeds put in trust and paid to listed charities including The Royal Women's Hospital, The Victorian Blind Institute, The Children's Hospital and the Talbot Colony for Epileptics'.

My mother died shortly after her seventy-ninth birthday and at the same age Flora left this world. Daphne had died when I was almost eight. As the only child and beneficiary of Mum's estate, the responsibility for disposing of 'Ponsonby' sat with me. Four generations had lived under this roof, from the Great Depression, continuing through the upheaval of World War II, and the promise of exciting change from the sixties through to the nineties. The task of clearing and preparing it for sale, as directed by Equity Trustees, was enormous. Without the help of John, my closest cousin back then, it would have taken weeks to complete. So many stories, secrets, awful events, agonising decisions and suppressed dreams were hidden in the very fabric of Ponsonby. The dark, antique timber furniture I had grown up with held a corner in every room and fought to remain in place.

My mother was sentimental, and we found she'd held on to piles of old greeting cards, sepia photographs and various other memorabilia. My duty as a loyal daughter was to pack away the lives of these characters. My emotional and physical exhaustion was such that by the end of two weeks, going there every day from 8.00 am to 6.00 pm, I could not make one more decision about what to keep, what to toss, what to donate or what to rehouse. Unable to destroy our history, I stuffed all the unexamined packages, albums, letters, diaries, as well as a battered old leather case found sitting on cross beams in the attic roof, into boxes and drove them home. Then I packed them away into the storage space at the rear of my garage.

Now, a quarter of a century later, it was time to tackle them again.

~

If Sarah hadn't encouraged me, I probably would have procrastinated until the days before the first open house, then ordered in a skip and dumped the lot. For decades, there has been resistance deep within me about looking into family history. I haven't felt a need and have been okay with sitting in the blank space. I have no desire to read my mother's diary entries or letters. It feels intrusive, disrespectful even.

Reluctantly, I open the back door and as I step out a whoosh of heat hits my face and I want to cry. There are Mum's rose bushes that I'd carefully dug up from Ponsonby and replanted here because I couldn't bear for them to be destroyed. That was a thirty-eight-degree day, too. She loved her roses, especially Papa Meilland, Dad's favourite, remembered for its large, fragrant, velvety, deep-red blooms. I've managed to nurse the bush through the past twenty years, but it won't be coming with me this time.

I head toward the built-in barbecue and images of my now ex-future-husband and his daughters pop up as a slide show might, some good, many not so good. We bought this place in Heidelberg together in 1992. It was the house I hoped would become the home I'd marry from and raise a family in. I was sold on it as soon as I saw it sitting proudly on the elevated side of the street. From my study and the living area windows, I can see over rooftops almost to the Christmas Hills over thirty kilometres away on the horizon. I feel most comfortable and safe when I can gaze out of a window and keep an eye on the path up to the front door. I've been doing it for as long as I can remember. This habit goes hand in hand with needing to sit with my back to a wall in a restaurant, or anywhere, for that matter. I've never liked surprises.

Matthew moved out for the final time in 1999. His decision, not mine. Thirteen years, a broken engagement, my skill at keeping the shame of the detail hidden. There's no reason to stay here. It was never a happy home and I'm drawn to moving out of Melbourne. I need a complete change as I adjust to life after Chris.

Now, I'm standing in the garage looking at the cupboards along the back wall, wondering what I'll find behind those doors. All I can do is keep repeating the same phrases to myself.

It has to be done. You have to unlock those doors. You have to open them. You have to bring out the boxes. You cannot take them with you. It will not serve you to move them from A to B again. You have to open them and sort the contents. You have to deal with whatever it is you find. Now is the time. You cannot move on. You cannot possibly reinvent yourself, heal the grief and loneliness, forget the failed relationships and create a new life if you don't. Now is the time.

There are three doors and three latches with three locks to this storage space at the southern end of the garage, reaching from the floor to the extra-high ceiling. The west side is open to the weather. I'll need to find a stepladder to reach the container that will likely contain what Sarah is hoping I'll find. The shelves are deep, and I have to lean in to get to the boxes pushed to the back. Years of dirt and dust have blown onto the shelves, enveloping their load in a gritty protective film. I'm regretting agreeing with Sarah to do this.

It's stifling, I'm perspiring and I'm pulling out the boxes that at some point I've had the foresight to label. With one huge breath, I reach up and find the aging leather of the old suitcase. I grab the corner and shuffle it into view, checking for spiders, then slide it toward me. The worn tan surface with its strap-wrapped mid-torso could not be more different to the pull-along luggage of today's travellers.

I hug it to me as I climb down and together we head out to the table so I can't inhale anymore dust and surprises. On closer inspection, I remember it's the valise that came with Dad to Australia. Clicking the latch carefully, I'm thinking this won't take long to sort through. When I see how jam-packed it is, my heart sinks.

This is going to be a lot tougher than I ever, ever imagined it to be.

CHAPTER 8

Lifetraps

It's 2010, and Chris and I are sitting at the dining table. Kev, the Burmese cat we adopted, is ambling round our legs hoping for attention. As cats go, Kev is a big personality and behaves like a dog, often darting to the front door when he hears a car in the driveway. Chris and the cat-dog have a special bond. Kev will fold himself around Chris's shoulders while they read the paper or work in the home office together.

I no longer live here. It's Sunday morning and we're back from doing one of the favourite things we still do together, a mountain bike ride followed by a hearty discussion over coffee. If you peered through the window right now, you'd think we were a happy couple spending our weekend relaxing together. What you can't see is the backstory of our relationship break down. I don't love this current version of us, but I have accepted the friendship we have salvaged. At least I still have Chris in my life.

~

Watching you making coffee, Chris, I silently remember our first meeting. It was February 2001. I was the 'Head of Career Services' for a start-up HR Consulting business and had joined the CEO on a sales visit. It was our first business appointment together. She walked and spoke with the air of confidence that often escaped me when I was in the presence of self-belief. You were the Managing Director we had come to meet.

I took a couple of steps back behind her as you strode into the meeting room, right hand outstretched in a welcoming greeting. I remember noticing your broad shoulders and upright stance.

'Chris Milne,' you said clearly.

Pause. Your eyes shifted to me.

'Michelle Scheibner,' I said, leaning into your proffered hand.

Our palms met web to web, equally balanced vertically. Your clasp was firm and definite, a signal to me that you knew exactly who you were and what you wanted from this exchange.

'Thank you for making the trek out to our humble business,' you said, inviting us to take a seat at the table.

You smiled as you carefully pronounced each word perfectly. Behind the lens of your glasses, your eyes were the colour of light-washed denim. It was a late summer day and the sun formed swaying shadows on the wall behind you.

As I listened to you give the overview of the business, my attention skipped from the dashing silver tips of your trimmed hair to the crisp, white business shirt with French cuffs folded twice to the elbow, each a perfect replica of the other. I guessed the cufflinks were safely stowed in your office, along with your suit jacket. Your tie, blue with a subtle geometric pattern, was tied expertly. You had the poise and professionalism of an executive used to the boardrooms of international companies.

Who were you? What was your story? I wondered. *Why was someone with your leadership presence working in the oldest, family-run SME business in Victoria rather than a substantial corporate organisation?*

You took notes with a black Mont Blanc fountain pen. Before applying the nib to paper, your arm bent with purpose, at right angles to the surface of the table and the royal-blue inked script tattooed the page with ease. I've seen this writing style a thousand times since. On our trip to Europe, you would hold that pen up with its namesake peak in the background as I captured the memory in a photo.

Finally, it was my turn to contribute to the discussion. As you studied me curiously, I felt comfortable and competent under your gaze. I knew my stuff and I felt in that moment that you knew I knew. Your employees would be safe in my hands. And then, in the next moment, you pushed your chair back with intent as you returned to your full six-foot-two height, announcing a walk through the factory. We won the business.

~

Our relationship had blown apart a few years before today's bike ride. It was a petty argument over whether I'd locked the back door. Chris insisted on how an acceptable apology should be worded and delivered. I failed his test. After several days of zero communication, I'd had enough of blow ups like these and his refusal to discuss them. I packed my stuff while he was at work and left. Weeks of silence rolled into months, then his surprise phone call led us to reconnect. He kept me at arm's length whilst keeping me close. But the intimacy had vanished. We found a rhythm, speaking every day, but we never had THE conversation about why we broke up. I would ask, and he would say it was him, not me.

Then Chris met Jane. He was smitten and I was devastated. When he told her that his friendship with me was non-negotiable, their arguments started. Reluctantly, I became his confidante, and with every one of those conversations, my heart ached not just for his pain, but for my own. My love for him did not diminish. I stayed in this situation, supporting him, copping his verbal pastings when their dramas overwhelmed him.

Why didn't I leave Chris to it and move on with my life? I stayed because on his good days he was my greatest supporter and my 'family'. We still did every birthday and Christmas together. I knew the story of his violent childhood trauma. Despite the abuse he'd survived as a kid, he was a compassionate and committed 'friend partner' to me. And he knew my story.

This day, chatting over coffee, we're sharing our thoughts on a book we've both been reading called 'Reinventing Your Life'. Chris's intellect drove him to search for ways to understand his own behaviour. He's been seeing a psychologist who suggested the book might help him understand cognitive therapy. These authors and psychologists, Dr Jeffrey Young, PhD and Janet S Klosko, PhD, refer to our underlying schemas or controlling beliefs, as lifetraps. The book's premise was that when these beliefs are challenged, the benefits can reverberate through many areas of the patient's life.

Chris was excited to find a framework offering him hope of relief from the feelings and problems he'd lived with for years and he'd encouraged me to read it, too. I was 'stuck' in the twilight between relationship and friendship with Chris and blamed our breakdown on my self-defeating behaviours. If I could work on my schema's, I'd have a better chance of moving us back to relationship.

The book included a questionnaire to help identify which of the eleven lifetraps could describe us. Chris and I had done did the exercise separately and today we were comparing notes. The scoring asks you firstly to rate the degree to which it was generally true for you up until the age of twelve, and secondly how true it felt as an adult.

The first two questions were easy for me to score highly, especially the statement: *I worry a lot that the people I love will find someone else they prefer and leave me.* When I look back at all my failed relationships, I've always felt some version of this, including what's now happening with Chris. When he tells me Jane is bright and can discuss quite complex ideas with him, that familiar twinge in my solar plexus reminds me of my shortcomings.

I pick up the 'skinny latte, extra hot' that Chris has made me, and we click teaspoons. It's a ritual we embraced so long ago that we can't recall its origin. It signals the start of sharing nourishment and conversation together.

'I'm looking forward to this. Let's start with our highest score?' Chris asks, jumping straight into it.

I hesitate. *Should I tell him how I feel? Or will I drive him further away?*

'Emotional deprivation', I say, not looking directly at him.

'Don't you think I understand and support you? You know I care and I'm always here for you.' It's rhetorical. In his mind, he is all those things.

'Yet, you can't explain why you choose to be in a relationship with Jane rather than me!' I say again. And again, there's no reply. And again, I start speaking to ease the tension and shift the tone, like I did as a child when my parents didn't approve of the questions I'd asked.

I continue talking. We were both raised in emotionally cold environments. Unlike Chris, my parents were not violent either physically or emotionally. They were present but absent at the same time. My memories up to the age of twelve are patchy. There are no mind pictures of snuggling on Mum's lap having a story read to me. What is perfectly clear is waking up from an ether induced anaesthetic with my head in a bowl filled with blood and vomit and wondering what on earth had happened. Of course they checked on me, but I can't remember any loving gestures helping me to understand or repair. Mum's go-to comment was, 'tomorrow is another day. You'll feel better then.'

Chris tells me about his dad's temper and painfully describes the time his dad screamed at him to shut up before pushing his face down into the mashed potato and butting his cigarette into the adjacent stew. His mother was little better, not permitting Chris into the house after he'd crashed his billycart and ran home bleeding from a couple of teeth knocked out. She opened the back door just enough to pass a cake of soap to her young son to wash his mouth out and clean himself up before coming in.

Abandonment and Emotional Deprivation are the two schemas playing out in our adult relationships. Chris worries about Jane leaving him and I worry about losing him from my life.

In summary, Abandonment is described as the feeling that the people you love will leave and you will end up emotionally isolated forever. Whether you feel people close to you will die, leave home forever, or abandon you because they prefer someone else, somehow you feel that you will be left alone. Because of this belief, you may cling to people close to you too much. Ironically, you end up pushing them away. You may get very upset or angry about even normal separations.

Emotional Deprivation is the belief that your need for love will never be met adequately by other people. You feel that no one truly cares for you or understands how you feel. You feel cheated and you alternate between being angry about it and feeling hurt and alone. Fatefully, your anger just drives people further away ensuring your continued deprivation. Individuals with emotional deprivation have a loneliness about them. It is a quality of emptiness or emotional disconnection. These are people who do not know what love is.

During our upbringing, Chris and I both experienced parents who could not give us the emotional care that babies, toddlers, adolescents, young adults need.

'Have you told your psychologist about me?' I ask.

'Yep, we have many talks about you,' his tone was caring as he continued, 'she knows how important you are to me.'

Then why? I don't get it. Why aren't I good enough for you? These are the words I don't speak out loud.

Why can't he see that he's withholding from me now? And why am I recreating those same conditions of my childhood with him? Each time I settle for his evasive response, I feel the familiar empty space of long ago. Why did I accept Mum and Dad's story about my brother?

CHAPTER 9

Genealogy

It's early 2017, and Sarah is still gathering parts of my story, trying to understand the grief I've carried with me to her rooms. So far, the sessions have been centred around Chris and the ongoing dispute over his will, which has left me stuck in a constant stream of emails, defending his wishes against lies and accusations. My capacity to function productively is pitted against these daily challenges, and I can't find an emotional equilibrium. Today, I begin by telling Sarah that my heartache still feels deeper, older than the feelings I've been experiencing since losing Chris.

When I first spoke with Sarah, I was so desperate for relief from my melancholy and hopelessness that I was ready to just hand myself into her process to find a way forward. From that first call, I immediately felt I could trust her to stand alongside me whilst I took one step and another step and another step. Her gentle and respectful manner both encourages and nudges me to look in the rear vision mirror with curiosity rather than regret. Together, we're unpacking one of the many layers I've stuffed into the invisible 'backpack of life' that accompanies me everywhere.

She's asking about my brother and I'm trying to find the words to narrate a clean, guilt-free version.

Sarah interrupts my thoughts.

'What's going through your mind? Where have you just gone?'

'I don't know where to start,' I say.

'How about at the beginning?'

~

I'm transported back to 2010. I'm at April's house and we're having a glass of wine together. She's a recent acquaintance and is curious about my family history, possibly because she's been doing several genealogy searches for other people. She's also a very direct communicator and I'm waiting for the inevitable questions.

'Do you have siblings?' she asks.

'No, I'm an only child.'

'Why do you think your parents only had one child?'

She continues sipping her chilled sauvignon blanc.

'Well actually, they had a baby born one year and two and a half months before I arrived,' I say.

'Wow,' she interjects, 'that's a quick turnaround! What's the story there?'

There's a pause while I take a breath. How much should I reveal?

'Well, when I was a very young child, not sure what age, I found a photo of a baby and assumed it was me. My mother snatched it from me and said in few words, "No, this is a baby boy born before you and died soon after birth because he had blue blood."

"What's blue blood?" I asked her.

"You're too young to understand," and with that the photo album was firmly closed, the photo taken and secreted away somewhere.'

April's eyes are popping out of her face.

'Blue blood! That's ridiculous. I've never heard of that. What's blue blood?'

I shrug. It was never explained. April has five children, the two eldest both with the Asperger's syndrome, so I pause, weighing up whether or not to tell her the rest of the story. Will she judge me by the actions of my parents? She's still looking at me, waiting for the rest of the story.

'When I was in Year Twelve, I needed my birth certificate to complete the application process for university entrance and scholarship places. My brother hadn't been mentioned again and I accepted the story of his passing before I was born in the same way I had accepted my family identity as an only child,' I tell April.

My parents must have hoped this day would never come. The birth certificate was handed over reluctantly, wrapped in the silence I was all too familiar with. I felt their eyes searching me for a reaction, then they exchanged glances. Why was there such a tension in the room? I read down the page.

And there it was: *Sibling – Grant Phillip, born 19 September 1951.*

'He was born on (my cousin) Johnnie's birthday,' I said with interest.

'No response. And then it began to feel a little weird. There was something missing from this official document,' I hear myself telling April, 'There was no date of death recorded.'

~

As I looked at that empty square, then across, first to my mother and then to my father, I slipped back into being the child trained throughout the previous seventeen years to not ask questions, and as an obedient child I complied.

There are times in your life when you realise things will never be the same again.

'He didn't die from blue blood,' my father tried to explain. 'He was born with a condition called Down's Syndrome.'

Hundreds of questions were crowding my mind as I tried to formulate a response. My voice left me. There was a tightness in my jaw, my back teeth were clenched, and my lips stuck together as I looked away from the informant. My mind forced my mouth to open, but no sound formed.

After several minutes of awkward silence, I asked my parents.

'Where is he now?'

'We don't know,' said Mum.

Gathering myself, I pressed them for more detail.

'Can't you find out?'

'No, when a child is made a ward of the state, the parents' relinquish rights,' she replied.

Dad said, 'There's no more to be said.' and silently they both turned around and left the room.

For me, this was the final confirmation that marked the loss of Grant from our family system. He was never spoken of again and I assumed if they could not give me more information, then they had not seen him ever again. At seventeen, I knew very little about Down Syndrome, and I was not encouraged to research any further.

This disclosure sat heavily in my mind for many weeks. Even after I completed my final exams and prepared to embark on university life, I was left with a silent niggling. It persisted and morphed into an undefined anxiety. In later years, every time I found a potential Mr Right, I'd wonder about my capacity to grow and birth a healthy baby.

I finished my final year of secondary school whilst trying to process three pieces of life-changing information.

1. The condition of my brother Grant at birth had not been 'blue blood'. He was a Down Syndrome baby.
2. He had been made a ward of the state, put into an institution soon after birth, and I was the replacement baby.
3. There was a possibility he was still alive, but it was highly unlikely.

~

April is waiting for me to continue, and I tell her the narrative offered was that Grant was born profoundly Downs. The doctors advised my parents to expect him to experience many and varied serious health complications, most likely resulting in a life cut short around seven years of age. April is not surprised and agrees that the norm of the day was for the medical fraternity to advise parents of Downs babies to hand their newborn over as a ward of the state, at which time they were placed in the institution known as Kew Cottages in the Melbourne suburb of Kew.

We discuss the history of Kew Cottages, subsequently renamed Kew Residential Services, and its final closure by the State Government in 2001. We wonder if the closure goes some way to explaining the confusion I'd met over records back in 1990 when I had tried to find Grant for the Genetic Clinic testing.

She's fascinated with my story, probably because she has contributed some research to the genealogy searches for a TV show, and now offers to look for my brother Grant. Both my parents had long passed by this day, and I assumed the truth had gone with them. The evidence I had pointed to Grant's name being changed when he was placed in the care of the state, or had been unable to survive the fatal conditions he was born with. I accepted this all my adult life. What other details can I give her? I don't have a copy of his birth certificate, but neither do I have a death certificate. Fleetingly, I wonder if my parents knew whether he had survived. Other than the untimely statement from my aunt on the eve of Mum's funeral when she told me Mum had visited Grant at Kew, my parent's narrative had been no contact, no visits, no knowledge. The truth was eluding me.

April is on a mission though, and her excitement at the possibility of solving this mystery is contagious. Unexpectedly, I'm caught up in the search.

Is the Universe sending a sign? What truth will April find? How do I feel about my parents' decision? I hadn't allowed myself to dwell on any of these questions since Mum had shut me down years before. I was a single child with only three, much older, married cousins and seven kids between them, the majority living in other states or country Victoria. I didn't have the same sense of family connection that April had. Maybe I should follow my parents' example and leave it alone.

This search proves to be more complex than many April has undertaken previously. The Registry of Births, Deaths and Marriages cannot produce Grant's death certificate. Is this the clue that his story is still alive? The window is open, just a fraction. Although Kew Cottages has been long closed, razed to the ground for a housing estate, April has connections and is able to access stored hard files. She sits down and goes through them one by one. The best I'm expecting is a date and cause of death.

When my phone rings a few weeks later and I see April's name flash up on the screen, I'm expecting she's hit another dead end. My early enthusiasm is tempered by the conditioning of family silence to believe he's long gone.

'Hey April, how's tricks?' I say, laughing.

'I've found him!'

A new feeling is beginning from somewhere hidden behind my third eye region and shooting like lightning through my centre. In an instant, questions are dive-bombing my brain.

What does she mean? Has she found proof? A death certificate maybe? Has she found my brother living somewhere?

April's patience and determination have been rewarded. In a box stuffed with hard files, she's found a discoloured manilla folder with the name Grant P Shriber handwritten on the cover. A filing mishap by an admin person decades before, misspelling Scheibner, has secreted his records and changed the course of my life.

April continues, 'I've been able to trace Grant to where he's living now. It is a state-run, assisted-housing unit in south-west Victoria, Ararat to be precise.'

I'm still listening, but no longer in control of my voice, there is no sound coming. April continues with her news.

'I've spoken to the manager. His name is Stuart. He has your contact details and is expecting your call!'

Hold on a second! What do I feel? What should I do? If only I could ask my parents. Who can I tell? I have a brother—finally!

'Thank you, April,' I finally gasp.

'You can call him tomorrow and tonight we'll celebrate!'

My immediate impulse is to tell Chris. I call him and he can't believe the news either. We talk about what this means for me and for the remaining family. Despite wanting to tell everyone, I can't yet. I want to hold it close. It's my secret to manage now.

That night, April and I go to an Italian restaurant to celebrate. I want to hear her tell the day's revelations over and over. I wonder if diners at nearby tables know the decades old secret that has been solved today. *Do I look different? Do I sound like a person with a brother?*

Back home alone, I can't sleep. Just like the night seventeen-year-old me first heard the truth of Grant's condition, I feel different. It is a totally consuming feeling. *Does this news justify my unspoken fear?*

I try repeating '*I have a brother*' but even as dawn breaks, it still sounds oddly foreign.

~

Sarah has been quietly writing notes, patiently allowing my pauses without interruption. I've been talking for most of the hour, giving her the details of events as a witness might respond to a police investigation. Hearing my own voice speaking aloud is like listening to someone else tell their story and I want to interrupt and say, *'Why didn't you ask more questions?'*

'What are you feeling about your parents right now?' Sarah asks.

I note there is still shame because the details reveal their choice to give a baby away. I want to protect them and to do that I must continue to keep the secret.

CHAPTER 10

Evidence 1

It's April 2017. It's been a week since Sarah urged me to push past my procrastination and get into the storage cupboards at home. Her hope is that amongst the many documents, there may be letters or certificates that will help me paint a more complete picture of my father, Carl Heinz Scheibner, and his history. She can hear how limited my memory of him is. Not because it's forty years since he suddenly passed away, but because there are inconsistencies in my version.

When she asked me last session to talk about him, I remembered the day of his funeral. It was my first. I felt so young, but the first family death leaves you feeling suddenly more mature.

~

I'm sitting next to the silent grief of Esmee, my overly composed mother. We're in the front row of St Agnes Anglican Church, across the road from the family home 'Ponsonby'. He's been dead for six days and I haven't seen her shed one tear. She hasn't asked me how I'm feeling. We have not talked about my father. All my mother has talked about in the days leading up to this moment have been the practicalities of planning a funeral.

I wonder if I'm the only person I know whose father died before reaching retirement. I can't think of anyone. My friends all had younger parents. Did I bring tissues? I can feel a tear edge its way out from the corner of my eye. There won't be a father of the bride to walk me down the aisle when I marry, even though I have no potential suitor yet. Dad will never hear the laughing of his grandchildren—the babies I anticipate having one day.

~

As I'm telling Sarah about this day, I realise I don't have any anecdotes about my father's life before his marriage to my mother. He was born in Berlin, an only child—'just like you' everyone would tell me. He trained as an industrial chemist in Germany. His cousin, Hilde, who lived in Sydney, was somehow connected to how he came to Australia and toward the end of World War II there are photos showing him wearing the uniform of the Australian Army. By then, he'd met Mum.

Other than that, he didn't speak German in our home, and to my ears, he spoke without any accent. When asked, he always answered that he was Lutheran, although he rarely came to church. The family chatter for as long as I remember was that I was the spitting image of him. But as for his life in Germany, his parents, aunts, uncles, cousins, his schooling, he never spoke of these younger years. I believed he'd spent time in the USA on his way to Australia, but that, too, was sketchy. My everlasting memory is that he was always tired. He would sigh deeply as he sank into an armchair, as if the effort of the day was too much. These days I hear myself repeating this same habit.

~

Now I'm itching to tell Sarah about the truths I found when I finally had the courage to open that worn leather valise last week.

'So, I found the case,' I say, feeling pleased to have actually done it.

'I don't understand why I had to force myself to do this. Why is it so hard? What am I resisting?' I ask Sarah.

'Parts of you want to remain loyal to your parents,' she replies. 'If there are gaps in your memory, it's possible you weren't ever told, and they probably thought it was better for you not to know. This is not uncommon, particularly in that generation.'

Sarah pauses and waits for me to pick up the story.

'So, yes, it was all Dad's stuff in the case. Letters on very old writing paper, almost tissue thin, and other records on heavy formal parchment with elaborate scrolls and stamps and yellowing with age. There were some translations that Dad must have had done for application purposes I assume. Then there were documents like birth, marriage and baptism certificates for his parents as well.'

These were written in 'old German' but Google Translate helped me make enough sense for a few puzzle pieces to start taking shape.

'As you know, my father came to Australia on his own, and I never ever heard him talk about what he left behind. To me, his parents lived inside a small photo frame typical of the times that sat atop Dad's wardrobe. Grandfather was Ludwig Scheibner, and my grandmother was Elly nee Scheye Scheibner. Dad's only reference about them to me was how much I resembled his mother, and I've always held a place in my heart for her, although I'm not sure why.

I knew Ludwig was born in Berlin, but I didn't know his parents were Hungarian, nor I did I know Elly was Polish. She was born in Lobsens, Poland, and lived there with her family until she married Ludwig.'

Sarah has been taking notes and now looks up and asks, 'Were you able to uncover any details about Ludwig and Elly's families?'

'Well, this is interesting. I worked out from the documents that Ludwig's mother was Julia Steiner. So, I googled Steiner and it's described as a German Jewish surname. But wait, there's more. Elly's parents were Kaufmann Moses Scheye and Henriette nee Benjamin. Doesn't this sound like a Jewish family?'

I sit back, realising what I'm saying. Judaism is carried through the mother's line, meaning my father was born to a Jewish mother.

'I found a formal copy of Dad's birth certificate. Yes, he was born in Berlin during the First World War. The certificate was dated five days after his birth, and states, "the parents were both of Protestant religion". The copy stamped "Officially Translated" was certified and filled out by a nurse at the hospital. There was also his certificate of baptism dated July of the same year, but it remained untranslated.'

I must look perplexed, and Sarah gently prompts me to continue.

'Elly was only eighteen when she met Ludwig. He was sent to Lobsens for work in 1910. According to their certificate of marriage, in 1912 she was aged twenty and Ludwig thirty-two. Her baptism certificate is dated four months before their marriage, and shows she was baptised in the Protestant Church, converting from the Jewish faith. They married because Ludwig was called up for war to work as a government architect and was sent back to Berlin, so taking her a long way from her family in Poland.'

I sit back again and look at the clock. Time has passed quickly while I've been consumed by what feels like my own book of history.

'Why didn't Dad just show me these papers and explain what he remembered?' I say, almost pleading with Sarah to make it all right.

'Imagine what it must have been like for Elly,' Sarah says. 'Her decision to convert and move away would have shocked her family at that time. Elly made a difficult decision and sacrifice to be with her new husband. But she would have also felt shame and possibly regret at shifting away from her family both physically and spiritually.'

I immediately feel Elly's internal conflict. She was so young and I'm guessing had never been away from her family before. I wonder if my father felt it too and, therefore, was reluctant to talk about it even later on, in the safety of his happy marriage and life in Australia.

'I get it, but why didn't I ask more questions?' I look at Sarah,

'From what you've told me so far, you were trained not to,' is her reply.

I get it now … he learnt from her not to talk about such matters, not to ask questions. And I learnt from him.

Sarah and I agree that I need to do further digging. I need to at least try to find answers. The aspect that nagged at me most was the question of religion. Why had Ludwig's parents converted and why did Elly turn her back on Judaism and convert to living as a Protestant? Was it because she was so young and in order to marry a man twelve years older, she believed she had no choice? How did her family react? Was she excluded from them? Did she retain the practice of Jewish customs? Did she pass these on to her son, my father? Was Dad a practising Lutheran or was it in name only, because he certainly never came to church with Mum and me? Why didn't he ever tell these stories? When I befriended a Jewish girl at school in Year Nine and attended Hebrew school with her during our sleepover weekends, why didn't he tell me then?

The biggest question I have as I head home is, *if their papers showed them to be Protestant, why were they persecuted by the Nazi regime?*

As soon as I walk in the door after greeting the cat, I head to my office, jump on the laptop and do another Google search to help get a picture of the events between 1933 and the outbreak of World War II in 1939.

I read that the largest Protestant church in Germany in the 1930s was the German Evangelical Church, composed of twenty-eight regional churches or *Landeskirchen*, that included the three major theological traditions emerging from the Reformation: Lutheran, Reformed, and United. Most of Germany's 40 million Protestants were members of this church. There was criticism within these churches of Nazi racialised ideology and notions of 'Aryanism', and movements emerged to defend church members who were considered 'non-Aryan' under Nazi racial laws (e.g., Jews who had converted). I'm beginning to build a mind map of credible reasons as to why questions of identity were hidden and not spoken of.

This accounts for the certified name change documents I found in the case, dated 1938 and declaring Ludwig to be known as Denny. Elly had chosen the name Tanna. Google explained to me that the change in Christian names was, 'common at the time and was due to racial reasons ensuing from the Law of 5th January 1938 issued in Berlin by the Chief of Police'.

It had taken me a few days to work my way through the contents of The Case I had named Pandora's Box. The process has been overwhelming, and the inconsistencies confusing, so I put aside any ideas of further research myself until a later time. As I hold Denny and Tanna's papers again, I remember that I *did* know about their alternate names. But who told me? And if I buried this, what else have I forgotten?

CHAPTER 11

Living Single

It's 1992 and we're driving along a road running beside a railway track. It's well after midnight, so there are no other cars in the way, no drivers to bear witness. He slams on the brakes, the car screeches to a full stop and he's roaring at me.

'Get out of the car!'

'It's 1.00 am. I can't walk home from here,' I shout back.

'I don't care, just get out of the car!' he says, and I see only hate on the flushed face leaning toward me.

'It's not safe around here. Anything could happen!' I protest.

He's gripped my upper arm with his bruising left hand, at the same time leaning across me to open the door.

'Get out of the fucking car!' he screams, pushing me with such force that if I don't control my movements, I'll end up face down in the gravel. Choosing vertical over horizontal, I step out, and he speeds off.

Who have I become that this is happening to me? Shame anchors my feet on the ground as I watch the rear lights fade out of sight. He wouldn't just abandon me here, would he? I'm fully expecting him to return after he's left enough time to 'teach me a lesson'. But he doesn't come back. So, after about ten minutes, I start walking toward home. The potential for danger sinks through the shock and I pick up my pace. The only upside is that the walk will take around forty-five minutes, allowing enough time for him to be snoring off the alcohol by the time I get back.

~

It's 2010 and catdog Kev is lying across my lap, his purring motor a backdrop to the memory. I haven't told Chris the roadside story before. He knows many things about Matthew and how he kept leaving, returning, only to leave again. In the context of the Abandonment Lifetrap, this newly remembered story has a place. In that moment on the roadside, I was abandoned.

Chris's voice cuts through the purring.

'It says here lifetraps actively organise our experience. They operate in overt and subtle ways to influence how we think, feel and act.'

He continues, 'When you have the Abandonment Lifetrap, you probably feel drawn to lovers who hold some potential for abandoning you.'

As Chris reads out the *Danger Signals in Potential Partners,* I make mental notes:

1. *Your partner is unlikely to make a long-term commitment because he/she is married or involved in another relationship* (married tick).
2. *Your partner is not consistently available for you to spend time together, he/she travels a lot, lives far away or is a workaholic* (workaholic tick, lives far away tick).
3. *Your partner is emotionally unstable (e.g. he/she drinks, is depressed), and cannot be there for you emotionally on a consistent basis* (drinks and depressed tick, tick again).
4. *Your partner is ambivalent about you. He/she wants you but holds back emotionally* (tick).

As I do this audit of my relationship history, it doesn't take me long to recognise the pattern in my choices. They are date stamped with the countless occasions when I felt abandoned and alone after staying longer than I should. After the usual schoolgirl crushes, I met my first boyfriend at university. It was first year, and only one other girl from school and I went to Latrobe. We moved in the same circle until she shifted into residence, and I became more of a loner. Up until then, my life had been sheltered. I needed to do a lot of adjusting very quickly. My two older cousins were already working when I started secondary school, so there were no family student role models. My first boyfriend showed interest in me and soon I was infatuated with him and his family. So, it began. But after a year, the more his eye wandered, the more weight I gained. In my mind, the two things were connected. I could have ended the relationship, but I didn't know how to. It was important to be seen as someone with a boyfriend, even if I wasn't happy. After another year, he broke up with me.

By the time I was starting my first year as a qualified teacher, I was living with my second real boyfriend Pete in a share house near the university where he was still studying. My head was turned easily when he showed interest, and I found his parents caring, but was it love? He was commitment averse, and although it didn't feel like it was going anywhere, it was more comfortable in a peer group of couples than the single alternative.

Joining the staff at a school was another huge learning curve, and my focus shifted to lesson plans, yard duty and finding my place in the hierarchy of student management. The one thing I brought from home that helped me get me into a friendship group was the skill of playing 500. I was accepted into the regular lunchtime card game, and this gave me an opportunity to mingle with more senior teachers.

One of those was a man eight years older than me, a head of department, a year level co-ordinator and acting Vice Principal when required. We were bookends in that we were both tall, tanned and large framed with dark hair and eyes. He was also especially handsome, not to mention fit from playing competitive football and cricket, and was well liked in the school community. The room would respectfully pause to look up when he entered.

On the other hand, I was not at all worldly, quite the opposite, a naïve 'newbie' learning the ropes. I'd also battled with body image since the first time I looked at a photo of a chubby me at about age seven. My mother took me to Weight Watchers when I was eighteen and I lost a heap of weight. But when I found the confidence to respond to an advertisement, thinking I could earn some money modelling, the rejection came with feedback that I was too 'large boned'. The weight had since crept on again.

Although I was never a confident extravert, teaching seemed to suit me. I'd just turned twenty-three, was learning the ropes, had a silent crush on Greg and then in July, my father died unexpectedly. Pete tried to understand, but was unable to support me emotionally. Greg, on the other hand, sensed my withdrawal and went out of his way to check in, especially after the funeral when life was expected to get back to normal. We began sitting together on the bus to sports events or at meetings. Then one day he drove me back from a union meeting. We stopped at a park and kissed. It felt both respectful and passionate.

This was the first time I had experienced another human 'seeing' me as a desirable woman, not a teenage girl. And suddenly I was in a secret adult relationship. Navigating the clandestine nature of this affair was exciting. After all, my 'crush' really wanted *me*. I felt incredibly special, in a way I'd never known in my life before.

Affairs need to be hidden or people get hurt, so changes had to be made. The first step was for me to leave Pete and at the urging of my older, more experienced, 'married' co-conspirator, I moved out of shared housing into a flat on my own, in a suburb I didn't know. Chosen because it was on Greg's route from school to home, the location enabled him to come and go without anyone knowing or judging us. On the other hand, it was further away from my friends, Mum and places I knew at a time when losing a parent unexpectedly should have connected me back into the family. Instead, I was eager for this euphoric feeling to continue and believed it was up to me to make it happen.

My professional reputation managed to stay intact. But I didn't recognise myself or the ease with which I accepted I was a party to the deception. I found ways not to answer direct questions about my weekend plans, dating progress or why I was leaving a function early. I became proficient at answering a question with a question. Even a simple statement from a colleague like, 'You look tired and not yourself, everything okay?' became a potential minefield to be traversed with a white lie.

At that time, there were no mobile phones for late night texts. There was no email with a secret address to exchange messages. When I was alone, I was alone. When Greg was taken to hospital with a smashed cheek bone, unable to make the agreed post-football game meet up, I spent the evening in anxious tears, assuming I'd finally been dumped and tossed aside. When he turned up days later, I was cold and silent rather than sympathetic. When I tried to explain how confused and hurt I'd felt, my words weren't heard or understood. Then I said, 'I'm so sorry. I'm being selfish and I promise I'll handle it better next time.'

On many occasions when he couldn't show up as planned, slowly but surely my self-esteem and confidence were eroded. Periodically, I'd try to end this affair, but his declarations of love kept me captive. It felt better to hear those words than to envisage living on my own without his attention. I was so desperate to feel a sense of belonging that I was incapable of making logical decisions. At no time did he promise to leave his partner and family for me. No promises were broken as I allowed my weeks, months, years to slip by. Living inside an affair is sad, lonely work.

Listening to mournful music and writing melancholic poetry were habits I'd adopted as a teenager when Mum and Dad encouraged me to use the big attic space upstairs as my own retreat. It was once the 'no go' zone where Auntie Daphne spent her days. But later I saw it as a safe cocoon, high above the world going by, where I could watch unnoticed. I created a space with rugs and floor cushions, burnt incense while listening to Carole King and hoped my tapestry would be colourful and romantic. Now I was living another version of that. My coping drugs of choice were food and romantic literature. I'd devour lightweight paperbacks, longing for a life with Prince Charming and two perfect kids whilst stuck in a version that ensured my dream could never be a reality.

The cost was enormous. Mum eventually discovered the truth and, whilst appearing to tolerate it, silently judged me, although no more than I judged myself. Together, she and I maintained the secret from the extended family.

All those years from age twenty-three to thirty, when my weekends should have been about exploring assorted social groups, bumping into a potential life partner, getting engaged, married and planning a family, I was at home alone, making every choice around Greg's schedule in order to be available if he could visit.

As my thirtieth birthday approached, I admitted to myself that I had experienced few moments of true unbridled happiness in my life.

It had been a very contained life up to this point, with clear restrictions rather than a prompt to explore. This felt like an adult version of being the obedient kid in order to be seen and included.

A friend was planning an overseas trip in the September school holidays and asked if I'd go. Why not? I'd show Greg I had a life too! And off to Bali I went. As I stepped onto the tarmac at Denpasar airport, the odd mixture of frangipani scent with the burning cloves of the Gudang Garam cigarettes bombarded my nostrils and I felt an unexpected surge of delicious freedom.

This version of myself was desperate to untangle from the secret and unhealthy liaison of the previous seven years. I was craving to be seen and ready to welcome a new future. The Universe delivered on day one.

With my travelling buddy ensconced under an umbrella, I adopted my 'tropical-beach-getting-a-tan-at-all-cost' position. The spent frangipani blooms lined the path to my idea of holiday heaven. It was only 10.00 am local time when the chatter of English accents broke into this idyllic scene. With my head turned just enough to watch without being noticed, I saw him—tanned, good looking, laughing and looking my way.

The next twenty-four hours were a blur. Simon was in sales and gifted in the art of spoken persuasion. We quickly established a banter and had lunch together. The afternoon dissolved into laughs, swims, photos, with later plans for cocktails, dinner, and dancing. In a blink, I found myself in an emerging holiday romance cut short only when he returned to England and I to Australia. Still, it had been enough to pull me out of the web of secrecy and pain and nudge me forward with renewed optimism.

The letters and phone calls from Simon started when I arrived home with pleas to join him for Christmas that same year in England. Who gets on a plane for twenty-eight hours to fly 16,893 kilometres to spend Christmas with a man they spent less than twenty-four hours with? I did. It was the perfect antidote to end and recover from an affair.

What did I have to lose? I had six weeks' holiday over the Christmas summer break. It was a huge decision, but my risk radar didn't kick in despite hating flying and knowing no one else in England. In my mind, risk was traded for hope and possibility.

It was the best six-week holiday I'd ever had, with a special Christmas meeting wonderful people, seeing the sights of London and my first trip to Germany. When it was time to fly home, we were both in tears and I knew I had to find a way to return. Back at work and looking for a way to be together again, I applied for twelve months' leave without pay to live and work in England. However, with my plans in place, the letter arrived. Things had changed for him. He thought it was better I did not come.

So, I turned thirty without a partner by my side. By the time I mustered the strength to find an escape strategy, I was a lonely single, compromising my needs, allowing my boundaries to be constructed by others and fully accepting that I was not worthy of a mutually loving relationship and family of my own.

But desperate times call for desperate measures and the next week I boarded QF1 from Melbourne to Gatwick, England. From the airport, I headed to Brighton, Sussex, with no plan and no permanent place to stay. I'd never done anything like this before in my life.

~

'Mish ... Mish, are you listening to me?' Chris asks, 'I asked you which statements you gave the highest score?'

He's moved to the chapter on *The Experience of Emotional Deprivation.* I flick through my copy to find the page and my scores. Six equals 'Describes me perfectly' and five equals 'Mostly true for me'.

I need more love than I get. Six.

No one really understands me. Six.

I am often attracted to cold partners who can't meet my needs. Six.

I feel disconnected even from the people who are closest to me. Five.

I have not had one special person I love who wants to share himself with me and cares deeply about what happens to me. Six.

No one is there to give me warmth, holding and affection. Six.

I do not have someone who really listens and is tuned in to my true needs and feelings. Five.

I am lonely a lot of the time. Six.

'My total was fifty-five out of sixty, which equals "Very high", I tell Chris.

'*This is definitely one of your core lifetraps,*' I read out to him, rather than each statement.

I don't want to risk Chris assuming my answers are referring to him and have this dissolve into an argument. The landline phone rings, and he heads off with Kev scrambling off my lap and pounding after him. My eyes are drawn back to this statement: '*I do not have someone who really listens and is tuned in to my true needs and feelings*'.

What are my true needs? So many times, I've compromised my true needs in romantic relationships.

~

It was to be nearly four years before I returned to Melbourne permanently. I kept being drawn back to Europe, having amazing travel adventures in Morocco, Spain and Norway, and breathtaking skiing trips in the Swiss and Italian Alps. I worked in different functions, including HR, in different industries, from telco to finance to engineering, and at many different levels. But I still hadn't found a soulmate to start my life with, someone to whom I would be the most special and loved person on the planet.

One week after landing back in Australia in 1986, I met Matthew. I was still living in the suburb of my shame years and had come back to find a new neighbour. It was a Friday night and she invited me out for a casual dinner with her friends, and there he was. Another 'tall, dark and handsome' guy taking an interest in me. Once again, swept up by the attention he showed and desperate to be loved, I fell under his spell.

Matthew was recently separated. It had been only a matter of a few weeks, and he was very much in the apprenticeship phase of life after a marriage breakdown. I should have read the warning signs, but he was persistent and I was susceptible to his insistence.

'I think I should move in here,' he said, after only a few fast months.

'Wow, really, mmm, okay,' I was flattered and concerned at the same time.

'It makes sense. I can't afford a place on my own and the second bedroom can be the girls' room when they come.'

It wasn't a question. He'd decided and he continued pointing to where his furniture would go, without noticing my hesitation.

'Are you going to work again? It's Sunday and you were there yesterday!'

'You know I need to be on top of things and can't trust the boys on their own.'

This was a constant exchange.

The loneliness in this relationship was different to how I'd felt during the affair with Greg, but it was still present. Back then, I was safe within four walls. Now I found myself walking home alone after midnight, in a dodgy area, after being pushed out of the car.

'I'm sorry, but you make me so angry that I just lose my temper!' Matthew offered the next morning.

The measure of my low self-esteem was that I apologised and agreed that it was all my fault and I'd be reasonable next time.

Then the threat, 'If you keep nagging me about going to work or drinking, I'm moving out.'

So, I maintained the secret, kept the injuries hidden and did not tell a soul.

A couple of years later, driving back from dropping his kids back to their mother and a tense exchange between them, he said, 'We should get married.'

Not the romantic proposal I'd imagined since my teen years, but I accepted. Within a short time, my property was sold and we'd moved into what should have been a happy family home.

My mother passed away the year after we moved into the new house. The next year, Matthew moved out for the first time. The engagement ring I had designed to include family diamonds from my mother's inherited jewellery went into the drawer. Our engagement was 'off' and in retrospect, I shouldn't have been surprised. His controlling behaviour had escalated and, whilst the emotional manipulation had increased, the physical abuse had decreased, thankfully. To be honest, I can't remember how many times he came and went before moving out the final time. The point is, the house that I so hoped would be a family home brimming with mutual love and respect became a quiet, lonely place awash with regret and empty spaces.

Of the thirteen years with Matthew, it seemed more were spent living alone than together. But he would not shut the door, so a hint of future promise lingered until I finally slammed it shut. I was again left with the belief that I'd not been enough for a man to commit to a life with me.

~

Catdog Kev races Chris back as I flip through each Lifetrap chapter, looking for the sections on the origins of this schema.

'Listen to this,' I say to Chris, reading the definition, *'Your family was excessively close and you were overprotected. You never learned to deal with life's difficulties as a child.'*

I was definitely overprotected.

CHAPTER 12

Ashamed

It's autumn 2017 and there's a chill in the air as I take the short walk from my car to Sarah's rooms. I notice the gardens are changing their wardrobe in readiness for winter and I make a note to self to do the same. The days are already feeling shorter, and I feel like I'm running out of time.

'How are you?' Sarah asks once I've settled on to the couch and put the mug of boiled water beside me.

Drinking hot water is a habit I adopted long before I met Chris, when I was at The Golden Door Health Retreat in Queensland. I had been personally anxious and professionally over stretched, so a friend suggested a seven-day retreat was warranted. It was. This is the only tip I've maintained, though.

'I'm okay, but I have a nagging feeling of running out of time,' I say thoughtfully.

'Say more,' was Sarah's usual response when I made incomplete statements like this.

'Chris ran out of time, didn't he? And I can't shake the feeling that I should have done more. There's only one way that palliative care ends and I didn't see it in time.'

My words sound so lame when I hear them.

'Describe how you're feeling as you say that,' she says closely, watching my expression and movements.

'Running out of time feels familiar, like I'm making excuses for letting him down. But I don't want people to judge me. It's like what happened with Grant.'

Now I know there are tears fighting for an appearance.

Sarah waits and watches, giving me time to acknowledge the connection, then asks, 'I'm not sure I understand. Can you describe for me why you think you ran out of time with Grant?'

~

The day I took the call revealing Grant was living in a care facility, Chris was the first person to hear the news. I relayed how pumped April sounded to have uncovered the information that led her to solve the mystery. I didn't tell him about the secret panic I felt, rising from my gut into my throat with a shameful thought.

Does this mean he now becomes my responsibility?

My exposure to the condition of Down Syndrome had been minimal. All I had was my parents' explanation for their decision, based on medical advice in the 1950s. They were told there was little chance of Grant ever talking, walking or being toilet trained, that fifty per cent of children with Downs are born with heart problems, so, if they were lucky, he might be expected to live into his early teens. Children with Downs were considered ineducable.

What on earth do I do now?

It was still early the next day when April rang.

'Have you talked with Stuart yet? When are you going to meet Grant? I'll come with you.'

Question after question spilled down the telephone line.

'No, I haven't made the call yet,' I said, trying to equal her enthusiastic tone, before going through the fictional reasons for my tardiness.

'Go on, I'll hang up and let you get on with it. Let me know when we're going,' and then click, she was gone.

I call Chris again and together we agree that the first thing for me to do is to make the call to Stuart and hear for myself. It still takes me an hour before I find the courage to dial the number April gave me.

'Hello, Stuart. I'm Michelle Scheibner. You spoke with my friend April yesterday and confirmed with her that my brother, Grant Scheibner, is a resident at the unit you manage.'

'Yes, hello, Michelle. From what your friend told me, you must be very surprised, shocked even, to learn he's here.'

'To be honest, I'm still processing the news. I didn't know he was still alive until yesterday. My parents both passed many years ago and left me with only scant details. Based on that, I assumed he'd died long ago.'

Stuart goes on to give me a brief recap of the attitude of the day, including how many doctors believed it was their duty to encourage new parents to give their babies up because they wouldn't live long anyway.

'Your parents were probably advised to go home and make another baby as soon as possible!' he says with a laugh.

Yes, and they did, and I was that replacement baby.

To shift the conversation away from this awkward pause, and despite an inner nervousness, I decide to jump in and ask, 'When can I come and meet him?'

The response was not what I expected. Stuart hesitated, as if carefully choosing his words before continuing, 'Michelle, let me paint the picture for you. Grant has been living in institutions all his life, and, despite having good care, he hasn't developed language skills or vocabulary. He has little ability to express himself other than using the odd swear word.'

Stuart pauses to give me time to understand what he's telling me.

'Go on,' I urge.

'Well, he gets very frustrated and has frequent angry outbursts, making it difficult for us to manage him. So, I can't guarantee how he will be on any given day.'

As I'm listening and trying to absorb every word Stuart is telling me, the earlier doubts are gaining energy and self-doubt is creeping in again.

Can I do this? Am I capable of handling this?

Stuart continues as if he's been reading my thoughts, 'Michelle, you need to prepare yourself before meeting your brother.'

'Thanks, Stuart. My experience of Downs is minimal. Go on.'

He continues, 'When it comes to people, Grant has a very short attention span. The hardest thing for you will be understanding that he has no comprehension of familial relationships. He won't understand that you are his sister or what that entails, so, at best, he'll give you five minutes of distracted attention before walking away. He'll have no interest in who you are!'

Pow! I'm stunned. Hadn't I seen a report on TV of a young man with Downs happily working at Macca's and chatting to customers?

Stuart is speaking again.

'Look, I get this isn't what you expected to hear. The best advice I can give you is to think long and hard before making the three-hour trip to get here. You will need to prepare yourself because this will not be the happy family reunion you longed for.'

Stuart added, 'Be sure this is what you want, because it might be life-changing in ways you don't expect.'

He continued, 'Can I update our records with your contact details as next of kin? It's a relief for us to know there is family to contact in the case of emergencies or accidents.'

'Yes, please,' and again I spell S C H E I B N E R and give my address and phone numbers.

I thank Stuart and end the call, sitting stunned, gazing out the window. The excitement of anticipation draining away, I feel the same dead centre of apathy I had years before when Mum had denied me further information for a test with the Genetic Clinic. I had ringed the absence of information about my brother with a comfort zone. Why? Why had I accepted their decisions and the story they gave me? I've been an only child all my life. Who would I be now? Now there was a new piece of the puzzle equally draining as trying to process the silence and absence.

I needed to talk this through with Chris. I trusted his opinion completely, and he understood how desperately I wanted to be part of the fabric of a family community. However, on this matter, he was unusually unopinionated.

'It's entirely up to you, Mish. You've been waiting a long time to fill in the blank, so you don't have to decide today. I'll support you either way.'

Then he added, 'Know that when you're ready to go, I will be there with you.'

This was the nature of our friendship—everything together.

The next call was to update April.

'You have to go. He's family,' she exclaimed excitedly, if rather too forcefully.

April and I had opposite experiences of family. As a mother of five kids, herself a twin and with both parents still alive, I was not surprised at her response.

'Why wouldn't you go?'

The next call I made, hoping for clarity, was to my cousin, John. He and Grant share a birth date and he's more like an older brother than a cousin. However, there was no encouragement from him or his wife, Barb.

'It's up to you,' they said.

'But what do you think Mum would want me to do?' I asked like an anguished kid.

'It's up to you,' they repeated.

Thinking about it again, they hadn't been as surprised as me to hear that Grant was alive. Was there information out in the ether that I didn't know? Searching every corner of memory, I pull up a snippet.

Remember that call from Auntie Orm the night before Mum's funeral?

'I think it's time you knew your mother used to visit Grant at Kew Cottages,' she said. 'Your father wasn't happy about it.' And that was it. No further information was given.

Procrastination is a default behaviour of mine. When there's a very tricky decision to be made, I put it off hoping for new information. Maybe I'll wait for the photos of Grant that Stuart promised to send. Every day, I check the letterbox with anticipation. A corner in my heart believes seeing the photos will push me into action. Will I heed Stuart's warning and stay away, or will I hold my breath and jump in? Finally, after a couple of weeks, a small parcel lands in the mail.

I tear open the envelope and out drops a familiar-looking, bright, Kodak-yellow photo pouch. I can't get inside it quickly enough. Eagerly, I flip through the pile, looking for evidence, a likeness of my father. But all I see is the face of an older stranger. I feel nothing. I expected and wanted more than anything a glimpse, a hint of recognition of my father, some family resemblance. But there was none. The man in these photos was bald and my dad had beautiful dark thick hair. The face captured here did not offer any familiarity. Pawing over the handful of photos, I felt nothing at all, only a new level of confusion and crushing disappointment.

In shock, I'm numb to the situation. The whole sequence of events has sent me into overwhelm. I'm no longer an only child, but the news is shrouded in regret, guilt and shame of the generation before. What would my parents want me to do right now?

~

Sarah gently calls me back from inside my head and repeats, 'Why do you think you ran out of time with Grant?'

'After I spoke to the manager at Grant's facility, I was conflicted and confused. On the one hand, I wanted to rush to meet him, but on the other, I couldn't even set a date and time. I needed to learn more. I was looking for reassurance and certainty that I was capable of being the sister of a brother with Down Syndrome who had been institutionalised all his life.'

'Did you speak to anyone outside of family and friends to talk it through?'

'I made contact with Down Syndrome Victoria, hoping to find someone who had a similar story. But contemporary support services were for families with a child or adult in the home. I felt like a historical character who had time-travelled.'

I pause before adding, 'Before I knew it, months were passing and I still couldn't move forward.'

Until finally, I hopped on a plane and flew to Hobart to visit the one person I believed could help me.

CHAPTER 13

Museums

It's 2017. I still drive down Hotham Street to Elsternwick for talk therapy with Sarah every two weeks. In between, I continue to sort and pack and clear my house for sale, whilst I journal my way through restless nights of insomnia. I'm trying to be systematic, finishing one room before moving on to the next, and this works as long as I don't have to make a decision about anything that came from Ponsonby.

Today, I'm hoping Sarah will help me decide what to do with the contents of the Pandora's box that was Dad's old, battered valise. Auction day is getting closer, and I need permission to free myself of it. When I've found duplicates or miscellaneous pages, it has felt okay to assign them to the recycle bin. But I can't destroy everything. All I have are patchy memories, and I know my mother would have kept the lot. That's why this house feels heavy with history dating from long before my arrival. I'm torn.

What does one do with family historical records when there's no following generation or extended relatives to share them with?

Sarah has read my mind.

'I've been thinking about you and your father's mementos. How would you feel about donating the case and contents to the Melbourne Holocaust Museum?'

~

It's September 2015, and Chris and I have come to Berlin on the last leg of what he knows is his final trip to Europe, a trip he was determined to make. His cancer treatment began with a seven-hour surgery in June 2013, followed by the first assault of chemotherapy, which took us into December of that year. Each treatment took four to six hours, and we filled in the time talking, often about travel.

It's been two years since the surgery, and I was not surprised when Chris announced he wanted to revisit Europe. He spent many years travelling to Germany for work to report to the Board. He spoke fluent German and had formed a warm relationship with Michael, the chairman of the parent company, and Silvia, Michael's executive assistant. Chris wanted to visit them and their families to say a final goodbye. The cancer has returned, and Chris has made the decision to cease treatment so he'll be well enough to travel, though now his pain is becoming more difficult to manage.

We leave the others in Bad Uberkingen with sombre farewells and the unspoken sadness of the occasion. Knowing I have only a patchy history of my father, Chris has planned to take me to Berlin. By the time we arrive, his body is flooded with medicative drugs fighting the increasing pain, and I'm wondering if we should try to get an earlier flight and head home. But he is fully invested in this and wants to make sure I have an opportunity to find peace with this part of my story and we press on.

It's my first visit to the city where my father and his father had been born, where they had lived before history stepped in, and I have been caught up in my thoughts. As soon as we drive across the border from France, I feel the tension increase in my bones. I've been so focused on Chris's care that I haven't considered what we'll do when we finally arrive.

'We could go to the Holocaust Centre in the morning,' Chris says during dinner.

I hesitate. I feel unstable internally as well as uncertain physically and weak on my feet. I have felt this since arriving in Berlin and I can't explain it. As usual, I defer to Chris and reply, 'We could. What would you like to do?' with the emphasis on *like*.

'I think we should go. It's important for you,' he says, determined to find answers for me.

I don't think I can do it, but I agree because I'm naturally compliant, especially with Chris. The Memorial to the Murdered Jews of Europe is also known as the Holocaust Memorial. This is going to be confronting, but I may not have the opportunity again, so I take my reluctance to bed with me and hope for a better day tomorrow.

With the effort of getting here from the hotel, Chris first needs to sit and rest. I sit, too, and take in the enormity of the structure. The sheer size of the installation creates a statement about the need for remembrance and honour.

My search last night described it as being '*in the middle of the city and a place of contemplation, a place of remembrance and warning*'. It was designed by a New York architect, Peter Eisenman, and opened in 2005. While Chris recovers, I take the opportunity to wander slowly around and between these solid columns. There are 2,711 concrete stelae of different heights, and the area is open day and night, and from all four sides, so visitors can wander through and experience the spatial impact of the structure. The uneven concrete floor gives me a moment of giddiness and I lean a hand on the nearest surface. The resemblance to a graveyard is not lost on me. Once surrounded by the pillars, I can't hear the sound of traffic or anything, really. Yes, it's so open, but the abstract design makes me wonder what I could confront inside. Do I feel calm? No, but I do feel I can continue with the visit.

We head underground to the Information Centre, also designed by Eisenman. There are themed rooms and Chris guides me to The Room of Names. I see a bank of computer terminals and a sign that tells me I can learn 'The Fates of Individuals'.

'Come on,' says Chris, 'let's have a look!'

In this moment, he's back in full control and is more proficient with a keyboard than me. He types in S C H E I B N E R, and I peer uncertainly over his shoulder. It's a short list and I see:

Scheibner, Tana Elly (nee Scheye),
24 June 1942, Minsk, Maly Trostinec, killing field.

'There … it's Elly. That's my grandmother!'

I'm pointing and trying to remain hushed at the same time. It's bizarre to see proof of my own relative's fate. Although there is no death certificate, the header of this page says very clearly, *Memorial Book – Victims of the Persecution of Jews.*

As Chris saves the document to print later, I stare at the screen at the other names on the list, in particular, *'Denny Scheibner'.* I know this is Grandfather Ludwig, but I don't remember ever hearing the story about him changing his name.

'It has to be Ludwig,' I say, and Chris sends it to the print queue along with Moses Scheye and Joseph Scheye.

The question I can't find a credible answer to is why they were victims of the Holocaust if they were Lutheran?

~

'The Holocaust Museum in Elsternwick? I've never thought of it,' is my immediate response to Sarah. 'Why would they be interested?' I continue.

'Their archive section would be very interested and I'm sure they could help with translations.'

Sarah pauses and waits for me to process the idea. Then she says, 'In case you wanted to, I looked in their directory and the best person for you to speak to is Dr Anna Hirsch, Manager of Collections and Research.'

~

Dr Anna Hirsch's greeting is warm and welcoming, and I follow her upstairs to the Collections area. Not far from her desk, a dozen elderly survivors are seated on high stools at high tables, quietly working on translations of diaries, documents and other material that has been bequeathed to the archives here at the Holocaust Centre. These volunteers look at me with curiosity, and my own doubts kick in and run like tickertape across the bottom of my mind screen with the words, *'Do I have a right to be here?'*

I pull out the copy of Elly and Ludwig's papers I brought home with me from Berlin two years before and hand them to Dr Anna.

'This is the most recent information I have for my grandparents.'

She reads without comment and places them back on the pile.

Still feeling fraudulent, I continue, 'When I think about what I do know of my paternal grandparents, I keep coming back to this secret around their Jewishness. My father must have known because he was forced to leave Germany. Why was it never spoken of to me?'

'See here, where it states Minsk, Maly Trosenic June 1942?' she shows me, 'Maly is a village near Minsk in Belarus. During Nazi Germany's occupation of the area, the village became the location of a Nazi extermination site. Throughout 1942, Jews from Austria, Germany, the Netherlands and Poland were taken by train to Maly where they were lined up in front of the pits and shot. From the summer of that year, mobile gas vans were also used.'

This potted history lesson leaves no doubt that my grandparents ended their lives there. I'm still confused, and I feel ashamed because I haven't dug around this before. Compassion for Elly's life lost is strong but the mystery keeps me separated from connection to these two people.

'I suggest you take all these papers home and set time aside to write a timeline of events, starting with your father's birth up until his arrival in Australia. This will give us the framework to be able to tell his story, explain the memorabilia and know where it fits within the archives and possible exhibition.'

She walks me back past the working table with the files stacked high, waiting to be translated by these weathered survivors of the brutal Holocaust. They seem so vulnerable still, but I can see their pride in what they're doing. Over the years, when I've bemoaned the absence of grandparents, it must have sounded as if I blamed them. I still have a lot to understand.

I shake Dr Anna's hand warmly and head home to begin another difficult task. I wish Chris were still here to help me.

CHAPTER 14

Stoic Mother

It's 2018 and still too hot to be heading into another autumn, but it suits me. Warmer weather means longer days, fewer layers, brighter colours and the lure of the beach. I'm running early for my appointment with Sarah, so I take a detour and within five minutes, I've parked in front of Ponsonby. I cross the road to St Agnes church and walk down the side path into the Garden of Memory, a space created for parishioners to place the ashes of loved ones.

Mum was very active in the church during the time this was built and a memorial service for her parents was one of the first. It's fitting that this is also her final resting place. The small bronze plaques on the wall tell many family stories, ours included. I wish I'd planned this visit and brought roses to lay. Mum loved her roses.

'You look well,' says Sarah, as she greets me twenty minutes later.

'It's this colour,' I say, referring to the sunset-red top I'm wearing, which is deflecting the sombre feeling left from my remembrance stop. 'My mother's hallmark was pale pink,' I add out of the blue.

Sarah is studying me now. She's picked up something.

'We haven't talked much about your mother. Why has she come to mind today?'

~

My mother, Esmee, had her thirty-ninth birthday the year I was born. She'd had a life before meeting and marrying my father, but I know little about who she was as a young woman. The setting for her story, and the opening years of my life, was an Edwardian house in South Caulfield. She had been engaged to marry Bill. He enlisted and was sent to the Middle East but did not return, presumed killed in action. Mum stayed in touch with Bill's mother for years, even after I arrived, so he was certainly important to her. Mum's parents, Kitty and John, were known to me only through the family gatherings recorded on film, and their life stories remain a mystery. Kitty was born in New Zealand, John in England, both dying long before I arrived. As a mark of love and respect for Kitty, they gave me Catherine as my middle name, and Grant was given Phillip in memory of Dad's father, Ludwig Phillip.

Mum was the younger of two sisters. Her older sibling Ormee, my aunt, lived with her husband Jack and family of three boys, Max, Robert and John, on the same street one block along. John, the youngest, is nearly ten years older than me. As Ormee worked, John spent time with us. His two brothers, being older, were well independent by the time I arrived. John has been a presence and the only constant in my life, frequently offering balance and sage advice.

Those who spoke at Mum's funeral described her as a real lady. 'Very feminine and gentle, modest in her achievements, and certainly not one to look for accolades or recognition. She valued her wide circle of friends and was highly respected without fail. But she was fiercely independent, even to the end, which was a characteristic admired and respected by all.'

There was a calm and elegant serenity which drew others to my mother. Many would come to unload their troubles. After all, I now see she was good at keeping secrets. When my married and divorced godfather finally declared his sexual preference for men, it was my mother who showed compassion and support and, I believe, had been his confidante for some time.

The sisters were chalk and cheese. Esmee was the introvert and Ormee the extravert. No doubt my mother was more compliant, her sister older by eighteen months and a force to be reckoned with. Ormee was more combative, as was my father, and they continued to butt heads throughout my life. I couldn't understand the reasons for Dad's rapid-fire temper response with her, but I could see it made Mum very uncomfortable.

When Esmee came home from St Andrews hospital in Richmond with baby me, she stepped immediately into a full house and a daily routine of not only caring for a newborn, but additional responsibilities looking after her own mother until she finally passed away before I reached my first-year birthday.

At the same time, Mum was caring for Auntie Daphne who was unable to live independently due to incapacitating physical and emotional needs. And if that wasn't enough, she was managing a husband, my father, a man on edge who didn't ever speak publicly about his own background. It was not unusual to hear them talking and sharing quietly for a long time after I was put to bed, but the stories were never shared with me.

My mother was a dedicated parishioner in the church, lived the life of a respectable Christian woman. She taught Sunday School, was on the church flower roster, sent me to the Girls' Friendly Society instead of Girl Guides and actively encouraged me to join the Young Anglican Fellowship as a teenager. I obeyed because the sweetener was, if I went to Sunday Evensong, I could go out with the group after. She and Dad chose to send me to Shelford Church of England Girls' Grammar from Year Five to Year Twelve, which completed and rounded off my Anglican upbringing.

To say Esmee was reserved is underplaying my experience of her. On the day of Dad's funeral, we sat side by side in the church front row. The minister was recounting his knowing of them, and my throat tightened as it does when tears are just moments away. They weren't tears for me; they were for her. In panic, I reached out and placed my hand over her chilled and still fingers, offering the warmth of comfort and understanding. As if lightning had struck the steeple, she pulled away from me and my gesture of solace. No tears signalled her loss. She continued to sit in silent and constrained resignation.

For the next seventeen years, my mother lived alone in the same large house opposite that Anglican Church. She had not worked in paid employment since before I arrived, although she'd always been involved in volunteer organisations. She managed solitude well, became defiantly independent, but did not once speak of her grief. A couple of weeks after Dad passed away, I told her it was time for me to move back home, but I was met with a very firm 'no'. Perhaps if I'd insisted, I would have saved myself from years of living alone inside an affair. She and I shared a capacity for solo living, but were either of us really content with it?

The final decade of her life was also a physical struggle. The symptoms began with trouble swallowing and mealtimes became a choking hazard. Her voice weakened. She suffered extremely painful cramps and the muscles in her legs appeared to waste away. Then the falls started because she lost the strength in her core and the power in her lower body necessary for balance. Her determination saw her visit doctor after specialist, but a diagnosis remained out of reach. A right parietal brain tumour took her life before the mystery illness ravaged her body completely.

~

Sarah is prompting me, 'I don't know very much about your mother. How would you describe life with her when you were a child?'

'Well, as far as I can piece together, when they were expecting me, her mother Kitty was in her middle seventies with terminal stomach cancer. So, by the time I arrived, Mum was busy caring for Auntie Daphne, my grandmother and a new baby!'

'Do you have many early memories of your mum?' Sarah prompts me again.

'It's vague, but I think Mum was on duty twenty-four-seven looking after Daphne's every need because I recall hearing Daphne's wailing calls for attention. Just outside my bedroom was a door to a broom closet under the stairs. It was dusty, filled with 'stuff' like the vacuum cleaner, and the ceiling sloped down as it went back to fit under the stairs. I'd hide in there, sticking my fingers in my ears to block out the noise. I couldn't bear hearing Daphne's distress.'

Sarah pauses and is watching me. I've floated back in time. I can smell that hiding place. It's dark but safe.

'Just take a minute. What are you feeling right now?'

'I was frightened of Daphne! I was a very young kid, and I didn't understand the concept of disabilities, let alone what hers were or the limitations to her.'

I can hear the childlike defence in my own voice.

'Yes, that must have been confusing. How did it make you feel, though?' Sarah asks again.

'I can tell you what I think, but I have no words for how I feel.'

'When you think about five-year-old Michelle, anxious and hiding under the stairs, do you feel it anywhere in your body?'

I turn away from Sarah's gaze and look out the window, trying really hard to *feel* something other than frustration in my body.

'You know this is so hard for me. I can see me, and I can tell you I was really scared, but I can't describe to you how I felt about it.'

'It's perfectly okay, Michelle. These memories have been buried for a very long time and the feelings have had to be buried too. How did your mum comfort you?'

'I don't know. I can't picture her comforting me.' I know my voice is shaky. 'She must have, but I can't find a memory of sitting on her knee or feeling her arms around me or hearing her soothing words.'

Sarah lets me sit silently.

'Mum once described herself as not feeling at all *maternal* before she had me. Now I'm curious about what she meant. She was kind, but I don't remember feeling wrapped in motherly warmth. Nor can I recall one conversation I might have had with Daphne. I'm not even sure she could speak coherently. The best I can remember is that she was short of stature, stocky and her hair looked like it had been cut round a basin. Daphne's condition was never talked about or explained to me. I was very scared of her. In fact, being scared is a shadow that hangs over and through my sparse childhood memories,' I tell Sarah.

'Say more' she urges.

'I was scared of everything, Sarah. Dogs and cats, people with limbs in plaster, injections, vomiting, the doctor and any sickness, going to the dentist, strangers. To this day, I can't control my anxiety at the dentist or when I feel nauseous—my whole body shakes uncontrollably—and I can barely get any sound out to answer their questions.'

With that, I slump back in the chair.

For the first seven years of my life story, Daphne was the strange-looking woman living upstairs because she was not well enough or capable enough to live alone. First there was a baby who died shortly after birth, and now there's my mother's aunt who was so unwell she required constant attention. Daphne died in the bathroom next to my bedroom, in the bath. Hushed tones and tears kept me behind the door, trying to listen and wondering again, how did the blue baby die?

There is absolutely no doubt that my mother wanted the very best for me, her 'only' child. But from the time of my birth until I was eight years old, her attention was torn in several directions, especially to fulfil the responsibility for the care of Auntie Daphne in the attic room.

CHAPTER 15

Evidence 2

It's summer 2020 and I still love nothing more than taking a book to the beach and getting lost in an author's thoughts and imagination, while keeping an ear on the rhythmic movement of the water as it shifts through its changes of tide. Today, I'm planning to journal. After walking toward a rocky ridge that marks the end of the beach and away from distractions, I take a moment to sit in memories. The seaside vista, its scents and sounds, so familiar.

For inspiration, I'm using the journal Michelle Obama published based on her memoir '*Becoming*'. The note on Amazon says it features thought-provoking questions and prompts to help you discover and rediscover your story. The wrap-around sleeve on the hard cover promises '*it's a guided journal for discovering your voice.*' I'm hoping the process will help me bust through whatever is holding me back from finishing the timeline of Dad's life based on the contents of Pandora's Box, that old case.

Feeling the sun and absorbing all of nature's gifts of a beach is relaxing, and I notice my mind settling into the task. Some of the question prompts in the '*Becoming*' journal don't invite me to write with curiosity. Until this one jumps off the page, '*Where did your ancestors come from and what challenges did they face?*' I realise I still can't write about this with any certainty. I keep turning pages and there's another, '*What kind of childhood did your parents or grandparents have? How was it different from or similar to your own?*' Where do I even start comparing my childhood to theirs when I've never heard any recollections from my parents, and never met my grandparents on either side? There's only one option now. I have to leave my happy beach place, head home, get the case out and interrogate the contents.

~

The afternoon has disappeared into early evening. I take my Mac out to the deck so I can enjoy the zephyr as I read. When Dr Anna Hirsch sent me home to write Dad's timeline, I expected it to be a quick task of looking for dates to build a chronological history. I hadn't factored in what it would reveal, not just about what I didn't know, but also what I'd forgotten. Today has gifted me a story, albeit brief and patchy.

This is the story of the man who was my dad and his life before he met Mum. Like Grant's existence, most of this information has been kept as a family secret.

If only Grant was able to understand how he was connected to this story.

Carl Heinz Scheibner was born in Berlin on 23 May 1915, a year into World War I. His mother, Elly, was twenty-three when he was born, the same age I was when he died. I felt so young and inexperienced at that age, so I'm guessing Elly must have been deeply in love with Ludwig to leave her family behind and travel so far away with him.

The *'Becoming'* journal had posed the question: *'What major historical events affected your family—whether in the distant past or more recently?'* I had found that Dad's early childhood was spent in Allenstain and Dortmund, where Ludwig was sent to work as an architect for the Prussian government. But it took another Google search to learn the history of the day. It was during this time, when Dad was eight years old, that he had his first close encounter of war and its consequences. Dad and his parents were living in the industrial Ruhr River valley region of Germany when there was an uprising. It was provoked by deficiencies in the German coal and coke deliveries to France. The provisions were required by a reparation agreement between the two countries after World War I. The French and Belgian armies sent sixty thousand soldiers into the Ruhr region to extract the unpaid supplies, and in doing so, took control of key industries and natural resources.

The German Government instructed the Ruhr workers to go on strike instead of helping the French. This goaded worker-saboteurs to blow up bridges, despite knowing that if they were caught, military courts had the authority to sentence them to death. In late March 1923, French soldiers had killed thirteen workers who were actively resisting, and this became known as the 'Bloody Easter on the Ruhr'. The event led to further protests and sabotage, as German civilians engaged in passive resistance actively refused to comply. As a result, one hundred and thirty were killed.

What would each day have been like for my eight-year-old father? His mother, Elly, was so far from her family in Poland. What did she do to make sure her only son was safe and protected?

Ludwig was subsequently transferred back to Berlin where he continued working for the government until he was dismissed on racial grounds. Because he had a baptism certificate, I'm guessing there must have been documentation that classified him as non-Aryan in the eyes of the authorities. After that, Dad, aged ten, had to leave school. He had not only been born into a society dealing with war, but had witnessed and experienced the fear and uncertainty of an uprising. I can only imagine that the family was becoming well practiced at concealing their Jewish heritage.

Somehow, his parents found Dad another school where he went until leaving to undertake an apprenticeship as a brewer. This truth was rewritten for me by my parents painting him as a qualified industrial chemist instead. When he completed the apprenticeship in 1937, he was appointed as an exchange student to The Swiss Breweries, a large business in Switzerland. After the exchange, he came back to Germany as head of the beer-producing department at a smaller brewery in Offenberg, but was dismissed abruptly when the question of race came up again. The Nazi's Nuremberg Race Laws of 1935 made Jews legally different from their non-Jewish neighbours. So, were the Scheibners Jewish or not Jewish? I wish when I was growing up, I'd had my brother at home with me so we could have talked about this and urged our parents to tell us more about their experiences.

Other records I found show that Jewish citizens—even as babies— were required to be registered with the police. Dad had carried with him an English Translation of a Certificate of Conduct, stamped as Certified by the authorities, and issued on 28 February 1938, giving all the dates when he'd been picked by up by the police and his papers registered. I'm pretty sure I'd never learnt this at school when I'd studied Modern European history, but when I was Googling to fill in the blanks, I read that the first concentration camps were established when Hitler came into power in 1933. So, despite Dad's documents showing *'no punishment has been recorded against him in the police lists'*, at the age of eighteen he was imprisoned in one of those camps from July to September 1933, then again from October 1935 to January 1936. Why was this happening if he was also carrying a certificate of Lutheran baptism?

In a letter I found in the papers Dad carried with him to Australia, he says, 'I was convinced there was no chance of ever being employed in Germany again.' Other translated letters in Dad's valise included one from grandmother Elly to her cousin Siegfried Benjamin, living in Brisbane. She wrote, 'It's now impossible for him (Carl Heinz) to stay longer in Germany for one day … Therefore, we must resolve with a heavy heart to send our boy to USA now.' This is backed up in a letter Dad later wrote to the Attorney General in Australia, dated 8 December 1942, when he was appealing his internment in Australia, stating he was subjected to special persecution by the Nazis until emigrating in 1939.

There is a gap in those documents about what occurred from the time of his mother's letter and his landing in Australia. Evidence shows he did sail from Germany to the USA. However, according to an email added many years later from Dad's distant cousin Judith to her newly discovered cousin Klaus Scheye, Dad boarded a ship as a 'Refugee of Jewish origin' and 'ended up at Ellis Island, not being admitted as an immigrant to the USA,' and was returned to Germany. He then applied to come to Australia through cousin Siegfried Benjamin who sponsored Dad with the offer of a job in Brisbane. This permitted him to immigrate here, arriving in Fremantle, Western Australia in April 1939, then getting himself to Brisbane. He was twenty-three years old, the same age his mother Elly was when she married, and the same age I was when Dad passed away. A curious coincidence.

The following excerpts are from formal letters dated June–December 1938 and provide the only information I have of that time.

- In collaboration through the Jewish Welfare Society Sydney and Woburn House London, Carl Heinz gained a permit to take up residence in Brisbane on 17 April 1939.
- He found employment at Castlemaine Brewery as a brewer and started 18 April 1939 on an annual salary of 200 pounds (Letter of offer from Siegfried dated 23 August 1938).
- He then made an application on 2 June 1939 (from Brisbane) for his parents to come to Australia. A letter from the Commonwealth of Australia, dated 21 August that year, notified Dad that the application would not be approved.
- Then, on 31 May 1940, the year after war broke out, he lost this position at the XXXX brewery on account of his German nationality and Jewish descent. What must he have been feeling when, after having to leave his family and country seeking freedom and safety, this happens again? In Australia?

Having been denied employment, Dad was taken from the safety of his new home in Queensland and sent to an internment camp in Queensland. Internees from countries at war with Australia were considered 'enemy aliens' and people were interned and held in camps around the country. According to records in the National Archives of Australia, the aims of internment in Australia in World War II were to identify and intern those who threatened the safety or defence of Australia, based solely on their nationality even if they had done no wrong. The reason given was this would allay public concerns.

Carl Heinz Scheibner, my dad, never spoke of this time, at least not in earshot of me. Did my mother ever talk openly about the impact these two years in a remote camp had on him? No, she did not. But as I pored over the letters, something was stirring in my heart. The feelings of hopelessness so familiar to me, but for which I had no cause, must have been what he felt. The wrench of grief and sorrow I remember feeling at an age too young to have cause must have been how he felt, knowing he'd left his parents to a certain shorter life ending in an early death.

What impact did the isolation of being so far from home in remote rural Australia alone have on him? I knew all about how it felt to be alone. It was a feature of my childhood. A new understanding of my father was beginning to develop. Could the exhausted, tired and often silent father I knew have suffered a form of post-traumatic stress?

My father had escaped Germany in time to survive the worst years of the Holocaust, only to be imprisoned in the land that gave him sanctuary. Did he feel abandoned? I haven't been able to find any day-by-day accounts of his time in camp, but I have pieced together what I can from information included in his numerous attempts to have his internment reviewed.

After ten months of internment, a tribunal hearing was held to hear my father's case for release. The request was dismissed, and he was to remain in detention without any charge ever laid. On 12 April 1941, he applied for release again, and this time he included a request for the hearing to be held in Brisbane where Siegfried and all his supporters were. This was also refused. The application for release was based on mental torture caused by Nazi co-internees in the rural Queensland camp, causing him to have a nervous breakdown. Dad wrote: 'A Medical officer made a report, which should be in my papers to the Court.' Again, it was refused.

Going by date order, the next formal papers indicate he was moved to the Tatura Camp 1A in Victoria and from there to Internment Camp 4 M.D in South Australia. No charge was ever laid against him other than being of German descent. Yet he was stateless, having been deprived of his German citizenship by decree of the Nazi Government of 25 November 1941. In a statutory declaration that same year, he stated he was in need of protection. But a letter from the Commonwealth Attorney General dated 28 January 1943 deemed it necessary for Carl Heinz to continue in detention.

So desperate was he to get away from this daily isolation and ongoing bullying, he tried everything possible, including requesting volunteer service with the US Forces. This, too, was rejected. However, in May 1943, Dad was paroled from internment into the Australian Civil Aliens Corps. The next year, he volunteered for the Australian Army and served continuous full-time War Service from March 1944 until

December 1946. His exit papers list a scar on his right shoulder. An assault, perhaps? Carl Heinz became a naturalised citizen of Australia on the 5 June 1946.

Who had my father become by the time he met my mother Esmee? I'm not even sure of the circumstances of their meeting as, again, it was never a dinnertime family conversation. I believe she was a Red Cross volunteer providing company to soldiers on leave and away from family, but I can't be sure.

Based on the contents of Dad's Pandora's Box, the history of two generations from inside formal documents has been revealed. But deep down I remained conflicted about my heritage. I'm positive I did not know any of this as a child or a teenager. There was no mention of Jewish relatives or internment in the eulogy given at Dad's funeral. However, I did know his cousin Hilde was living in Sydney and I do remember her family being described as 'Liberal Jews'. There was only spasmodic contact between them, although when Dad died and Hilde lost her husband, the two widows grew closer.

How did I fail to make the connection to a Jewish heritage in a conscious way? If I could have a conversation with him, I'd ask him why he continued to maintain the secret long after the war ended.

Dad was thirty-eight years older than me and of another generation, another time, another culture. I have absolutely no doubt that he loved Mum and me dearly. Despite that, my memory of childhood is one of a little girl feeling sad, very sad, preferring to be alone than to be in the company of her forlorn parents. He passed away suddenly, without warning, in what we called the Breakfast Room at Ponsonby. Mum found him. Theirs was a story of finding love when both had lost any expectation of happiness. Despite this, he died sad and exhausted from the effort of life at only sixty-two. The words of Poet Laureate Maya Angelou say it all.

"There is no greater burden than carrying an untold story."

CHAPTER 16

Another Funeral

It's Monday, 30 September 2014. Chris and I shiver as the wind pushes us toward the open doors. There's a different stillness in a church before a funeral, a slight murmur, some organ music. I pause just inside the door before introducing myself to the representative of the funeral home. In place of a large floral tribute, there are branches from a tree placed in an urn. Perched up in the branches is a bright purple knitted teddy bear, facing out toward the congregation. Curious. It's like a setting for a child's funeral.

The drive today to the Victoria country town of Stawell has been sombre. Chris insisted on driving me despite being mid cycle of his first chemotherapy treatment. He understands the enormity of the day. As my immediate confidant, he'd ridden shotgun to the events that had brought me to this church.

I'm nervous, and in retrospect, driving myself probably wouldn't have been my smartest option. I have no idea how I'm going to introduce myself. I don't know who will be here, or how they will treat me when they realise who I am. I'm walking into a completely unknown situation; one I couldn't have possibly imagined five years ago. I certainly hadn't anticipated this local church bursting with so many people wanting to say a final goodbye to Grant.

I hadn't prepared for how the words would stick in my throat when I tried to speak. I hear a familiar voice say, *I'm Michelle Scheibner, Grant's sister,* but it sounds disconnected from me, as if I'm lying. Referring to a brother is so unpractised and foreign.

The funeral director walks us down the centre aisle to the first row, past strangers who are smiling at me sympathetically. So many people are here! As an immediate family member, I'm entitled to sit at the front, as I had for Dad's funeral and for Mum's. I hope I have enough tissues in my bag to see this through.

I don't sense a shroud of grief, other than my own. The coffin appears shorter than you'd expect for an adult and is positioned ready for the service to begin. If I stood up and stretched out my arm, I could almost touch it. As a distraction, I focus on the details around me. It's the original style Anglican Church typically built in the 1890s, with ceilings up to the heavens. The layout of the chancel is familiar, with an altar and a pulpit raised above the surrounding floor. The lectern, holding an oversized bible, is ready for the readings.

I wonder why an Anglican Church was chosen. A lucky guess, or did they somehow know?

Now I stare straight ahead so as not to make eye contact with those people slipping into the pew beside me. I'm waiting for the service to be over.

~

It was nearly two weeks ago when I received the call. I had been in my home office for a couple of hours, catching up on work emails, when the landline rang. I assumed it would be Chris reminding me of his oncologist appointment that afternoon.

'I am looking for Michelle Scheibner,' an unknown male voice said.

'Speaking,' I replied.

'Ah, good, my name is James Roberts and I'm with State Trustees Victoria. It is my duty to notify you that your brother, Grant Phillip Scheibner, passed away last night in Ballarat hospital.'

His words sucked the breath out of me and an electric shock ran from my gut into my throat. Then, within an instant, I was ice cold. James continued, telling me he had some difficulty in finding any next of kin. He asked me to spell my name just to make sure he had the correct person. I was stunned. The agreement I had with Stuart, the manager at Grant's facility, was that his records were to be updated with my contact details as next of kin. I had very carefully spelled out S C H E I B N E R to him. This was to ensure that should there be any health issues or concerns, I would be contacted immediately. Why had it been so hard for James to track me down?

Finding my voice again, I said, 'His carers have my details. Why wasn't I informed directly?'

'There was no record of relatives or any contact details, which is why it came to my department,' James replied patiently. He sounded accustomed to difficult conversations.

Are you kidding me? I rant to myself, before hitting him with questions. How long had Grant been unwell? How long in hospital? What were the symptoms? Diagnosis? Who was with him?

'I'm sorry, Michelle, I don't have any of that detail. When I let the unit manager responsible for Grant's care know I have found you, I'll ask him to give you a call.'

'Thank you, James. I have one last question. What happens now? Do I organise the funeral?'

The man from State Trustees explained that, as Grant was made a ward of the state as a baby, he was supported by an invalid pension. Those funds were used to arrange a prepaid funeral. There would be a church service, followed by a private cremation, and his ashes would be placed in an unmarked area of the local Memorial Garden in Stawell.

'I'm sure Nick will be able to give you all the necessary details.'

I was confused, 'Nick? Who's Nick? I spoke to someone called Stuart. Where's he?'

James had hung up and I could only hear the dial tone. I'd been planning to call cousin John to wish him a happy birthday, but that could wait. Now wasn't the time. Instead, I silently wished Grant was still alive to celebrate his birthday rather than dying on the eve of turning sixty-three. There was something lurking in my mind about that age. What was it?

~

Now, at the funeral service, the Anglican Minister is eloquent and warm as she delivers the eulogy for a stranger. She doesn't mention Grant's family but gives an account of his life based on the chats she's had with the team who looked after his every need. It's an unexpectedly loving service and yet my grief is fuelled by the complexity of my parents' loss.

'Grant loved his collection of teddy bears, and this fella was a favourite,' she tells us, pointing to the purple teddy in the tree branches.

'He had quite a collection and took at least one with him everywhere, often misplacing them. Grant's anxious searching signalled to his carers to look out in the yard, especially up in the trees, where he liked to hide them.'

This brought a knowing murmur from everyone around me. How ironic that my brother had a collection, but as a child I had only one special teddy, previously owned by John. Despite living into adulthood, Grant had never stopped being a young boy.

At the end of the service, a casually dressed man, aged around forty, introduced himself as Nick, the manager of the facility, who I'd spoken with a couple of weeks ago, soon after the call from James. During our conversation then, Nick mentioned the plan was to have a small wake after the service and I was most welcome to join them. Chris is keen for us to use the opportunity to find out what had happened to Stuart. What had happened to my contact details? Why had no one called me when Grant first became ill?

~

The facility is a brown brick house surrounded by a neat garden. There is no signage. I look in the letterbox and find a business envelope with a clear panel, so I can see it's addressed to Grant. S C H E I B N E R is spelt correctly. So why has it been this hard to find me?

'Nick didn't have to invite you,' Chris says. 'He seems interested and knows this is important. Don't be embarrassed to ask questions. It's going to be okay.'

We follow the chatty voices coming from a space toward the back of the house. It's a large living area adjacent to the small kitchen, with a dining table laden with sandwiches and scones typical of country hospitality.

Everyone looks at ease, talking comfortably, but my introversion kicks in, along with my guilt, and I search for Nick so he can introduce me to the group and explain why I'm here. I needn't have stressed. There is no judgement, just a bunch of dedicated care workers who want to share their stories of Grant with me. I move amongst the group, juggling a cup of tea and forcing myself to say the words out loud, 'I'm Michelle, Grant's sister.' It becomes apparent that, despite his physical and cognitive limitations, Grant had a distinct personality with a sense of fun. He had a love of playing drums and watching the wrestling and slapstick comedy. His favourite thing was hours of cricket coverage.

Just like his dad!

I had brought with me the only photo of Grant I owned, as well as photos of Mum and Dad. Every person in the room was interested and all said they could see the resemblance to Dad.

'Grant hadn't changed much since he was a baby!' is the popular opinion. I ask about his speech and attention span and Jodie, one of the carers, explains that being institutionalised from such a young age with other similar children, he hadn't developed language early enough and couldn't express himself with words. He'd draw attention to his needs with gestures and sounds. She giggles as she tells me his only language was two words: *sausages* and *shit*! No one mentions the anger management difficulties Stuart spoke of four years ago.

Nick takes me aside.

'Would you like to see Grant's room?'

The bedroom has posters on the walls and several framed photos of other residents, carers and friends. Grant had owned a camera, I was told. He loved photography and had taken these pictures himself. It feels like a room of a teenage boy, except for the collection of teddy bears. There's a hospital bed with a soft padded mat on the floor beside it and a pair of slippers. Grant must have had tiny feet. Nick explains the mat was to break his fall should he tumble out during the night. He explains how Grant had suffered from chronic heart issues for many years, and more recently, dementia, hence the hospital bed and floor protection. Grant had very high cholesterol when he first came to Navarre House two years ago, but that had been reduced. He also had a problem with his eyes and outdoor light had become an issue.

'Nick, can you tell me what happened at the end?' I ask. 'Was he alone in hospital?'

Grant's final stay in hospital had begun with pneumonia, a common result of the multiple conditions he had. In the end, his heart failed. Nick visited him every day and was the one to make the formal identification.

The description of the end to Grant's life is heartbreaking. My brother had lived in a parallel universe to me and now I'm standing in his world, in his most personal space. In this moment, I see Grant as more than a name on my birth certificate. He has an identity, with layers, with a story. But his story doesn't include a sister, or a mother or father. Like me, his story didn't have grandparents.

I take the opportunity to ask Nick about the puzzle of the missing next of kin details.

'I don't know what happened to the file note of your call to Stuart. There was nothing in Grant's records to show anyone had spoken to you, or about your request to visit.'

I'm dumbfounded.

Nick continues, 'In fact, I was unaware that Grant had a sister until James from State Trustees phoned.'

I relate the conversation I had with Stuart in 2010, the day after April found Grant was on file here. Nick is apologetic, and I press him for an explanation.

'Stuart had already left the department when I started, so while I personally have no idea what happened, one hears things but I can't honesty tell you.'

He goes on to explain how excited they all are when lost relatives are discovered. Their processes allow Nick's team to go to great lengths to accommodate the needs of all parties involved to expedite reunion visits, including taking the resident to the family, if needed. Had it been Nick I spoke to originally, I believe I would have met Grant.

Nick and I head back out to the gathering, and I see Chris having an animated chat with a tall woman dressed in a charcoal grey uniform of pants, shirt and matching jacket. Chris introduces her as Libby,

Grant's carer.

Grant was Libby's favourite. She'd known him since she did a placement twenty years ago at Pleasant Creek, another institution. She explains that when Kew Cottages closed, administrators went to great lengths to find relatives so they could jointly decide about ongoing care. The records must have shown that Grant did not have any next of kin she tells me.

'But there were only two Scheibners in the Melbourne phone book at that time. Mum and me,' I tell her, trying to hide my frustration.

'They can't have tried very hard!'

Or did Mum get a call? I wonder.

'Libby, how do you spell Scheibner?' I ask, thinking that can be the only explanation.

'S C H E I B N E R,' Libby says confidently.

Chris fills the silence.

'Tell Mish about your shopping expeditions with Grant!'

Libby describes Grant's good fashion sense, which I'm super excited to hear. He was particular about how he dressed, even insisting on making his own choices each day. He loved clothes shopping with Libby, and when she'd hold up an item for approval, if he didn't like it, he showed his disapproval with a hand movement. As Libby mimics the gesture, Chris jumps in again, 'That's exactly what you do when I take you clothes shopping for me!'

We all laugh at the tenuous connection.

'You know, despite his inability to speak, Grant was very compassionate. When a new resident named Xavier was transferred here, he was so insular we couldn't get him to interact. Grant persisted, and was the only one Xavier responded to. They went on to develop a firm friendship.'

Hearing this makes me smile until I remember Stuart's words describing Grant as angry and incapable of social connections. I'm relieved, though. Maybe Grant and I did have something in common after all.

When Libby asks if I'd like to see some recent photos of Grant, I hesitate, remembering the photos Stuart had sent, but she's already rushed off to get them. She returns with a yellow Kodak envelope, identical to the one I have in a drawer at home. She pulls out the same images that drowned my expectations previously, but as she hands them over, she says, 'Hang on, this isn't Grant!' and disappears. When Libby returns, I hold my breath and silently wish for a recognition miracle this time. I want my brother!

'Here he is. The other packet was incorrectly labelled!'

I grab the photos.

After sixty years of wondering about my brother, I finally see the family resemblance in the face smiling at the camera. This was my dad's son, my lost blood brother.

~

That night, back home alone, I see Grant's face every time I close my eyes. I run through every detail I heard today, no matter how insignificant, for now I have a profile of the person known as Grant. He's no longer a character in a search or legal document. He now has an identity and, despite only brief detail, I can describe who the missing baby became. The next day, I send a card with a note to Nick.

Wednesday, 1 October 2014

Dear Nick and everyone at Navarre Road, Williams Street and Day Programs,

I want to take this moment to write to you and thank you so very much for your warmth at Grant's funeral, and at the gathering after. It was such a pleasure to meet you; to hear your thoughts and memories; to see those photos and to come away with a greater understanding of the care and devotion you all have for those you nurture … when their families cannot.

I didn't know what to expect and I felt quite anxious as we drove into Stawell. Yes, it was an overwhelming day, and I didn't sleep last night. However, I now feel the circle is closing and I am at last finding peace with our history. You helped me find my brother and that is gold to me. Thank you again for looking after Grant and for welcoming my presence with you at his farewell. You are all simply amazing.

Warmest regards,

Michelle

This little baby who had been put away into a 'home' because it was assumed he would not live past his first seven years had outlived both his parents. As I addressed the envelope to Nick, the recurring niggle about the timing of Grant's passing hit me. I quickly did the sums in my head. Dad had died at age sixty-two, too.

CHAPTER 17

Love Story

It's early 2021. The sea has a sparkle and I take a moment to appreciate how fortunate I am to be living just a five-minute walk from the beach in Mornington. I find a sandy hollow to get comfortable so I can continue reading Eddie Jaku's book, 'The Happiest Man on Earth'. This is one of my favourite things in life, finding a space away from other beachgoers and feeling the sun warm my soul while I escape into someone else's world. Our family had a beach house at Rosebud on the Mornington Peninsula when I was a kid, and Mum kept a stash of romance novels for summer reading. When other kids were engrossed in adventures and play, at twelve, I was reading 'Gone with the Wind', imagining my life with a charming Rhett Butler. My literary choices conditioned me to expect a forever love story as the norm.

I bought Eddie's book after hearing him on a podcast talking about how he survived the Holocaust and made his way to Australia. Despite what he'd been through, he still described himself as the happiest man on earth, and I wanted to learn how that was possible. I look up from a paragraph about Eddie marrying Flore in 1946 and see a mature couple strolling along the shoreline hand in hand. They're not in a hurry, just chatting with each other, if I squint, they look just like my parents heading off on a beach walk. It's the same 'couple's body language' of familiarity that comes from years of intimacy. How often did I see this as a kid? My parents with an energy field around them, like a fort, and a little Michelle always walking a few steps behind, outside their space, and on her own.

It's time for a swim, to rinse off the disappointments. The chilly
saltwater stuns me back into the present. Chris wasn't a beach lover
and I've been making up for the time I lost when I went with him to the
Victorian high country. It was home to two of his favourite pastimes,
fly-fishing for rainbow trout and Nordic ski runs. He was so keen to
coach me on both, but I didn't attain his level of mastery.

After my swim, I head home to Pandora's Box where I've put two
neatly packed bundles of letters that I found in the move. One package
is tied together with old string, just as I found it, still unopened. The
other, in Mum's handwriting, is inside a large plastic file. Placing them
on the table, I notice again how small the envelopes are, how the
ink has faded on the thin paper. To read these safely, I need to shift
from daughter to researcher, from the past to the present, from guilt
to innocent curiosity. I want to understand why the term 'emotional
deprivation' that Chris and I discovered fits me so comfortably, despite
having two parents who loved me. They did not abandon me. They did
abandon Grant, though.

~

Like her mother, Kitty, and grandmother, Flora, Mum was an active
volunteer in the local branch of the Red Cross. She must have met
Dad through this involvement, as the Red Cross volunteers provided
compassionate services to the army personnel stationed in Melbourne
and away from family during the war. My father was one of those
servicemen, having joined on his release from internment. The dating
pair relied on letter writing and the postal service to stay in touch.
These letters are evidence of a bumpy start to their relationship.

The earliest letters I can find in these bundles are dated 1944, a year
before the end of World War II and three years before their marriage.
The timeline shows they met in April that year. Dad was posted at
a regional barracks, yet despite the distance, letters seem to travel
back and forth quickly. Letter after letter has a repeated theme of an
apology for an argument, mostly from Mum, and ending with a plea
for forgiveness and a declaration of everlasting love.

Mum was reserved initially.

'If I love I will get hurt. I had years of being tortured and came to the conclusion that one could be happier without real love. I have only loved once before. I know it can take me to heaven and hell.'
(21 April 1944)

I assume the source of her hell was not knowing what had happened to Bill.

'Something will happen and I'll get the sulks and you'll get annoyed with me.' (19 May 1944)

Ah, so getting the sulks began when she was a young woman. No wonder she was so practised at it with me. I always knew when I had said or done something she didn't approve of, because she would sulk and simply not speak. Mealtimes in silence at the kitchen table were often the norm and soon became my response, too.

'I had two apples and a banana for lunch. I fear the worst now. My weight will go up again.' (22 May 1944)

Mum was obsessed with managing her weight even then. The subject of diets was commonplace between us, especially after the ballet teacher told her I was too big to continue lessons. Our class had just begun en pointe, and I was delighted and felt very grown up. The news that I was too big shattered my confidence and at eight years of age I began watching everything I ate. I still do, and I still have my case with those specialized ballet shoes. The excerpt could just as easily have been written by me.

'I try to please you. I told you I would be hard to get on with. You see, I need so much convincing. I like you to tell me over and over again, over and over and then never stop saying you're mine.' (1 June 1944)

This tone began within weeks of their meeting, as did the issue of misunderstandings and petty arguments. She was consumed with doubt and the need for reassurance occupied her thoughts as she asks, *'will you love me forever?'* constantly.

> *'... You have knocked the bottom out of my world ... I am not jealous this time. It is the fact that you pretended that you loved me ... I hope tomorrow I will get a letter and you don't say anymore nasty things to me but treat me lovingly ... Darling ... tell me you still love me.'*
> (18 July 1944)

One year on, and they are still writing passionate love letters.

Mum tells Dad, *'Thank you, my darling, for coming into my life twelve months ago and for sticking to me and giving me such happiness and such a wonderful feeling that I am not alone in the world but that there is someone who loves me so much.'* (12 April 1945)

There is a stabbing familiarity in this letter. Mum was not alone in the world. She lived at home with her sister, brother-in-law, nephews, mother and aunt, yet she felt alone. How curious. My own words written several times over the decades of my life.

I notice the phrasing and 'complaints' in these letters of my mother's, with a tone of pleading for forgiveness after a tiff; evidence of insecurity and a repetition of the question 'prom*ise me you will love me forever?'* It's like a self-recognition in reading her words, tone, her submissive and compromising relationship language. She, too, was unable to set boundaries and state her needs in a confident and unthreatened way.

~

Dad's written English grammar improved with each letter, but even in the earliest missives I find hints of his state of mind and desperation for a normal life.

'I fight extremely hard against it. You know the reasons why, too, and please, my darling, have mercy with me. It is hard and the pain awful. The heart is bleeding and aching and I don't know how to stop it, so please, again, have mercy with me. I like you too much, but I can't explain the rest of my feelings.' (19 April 1944)

And then three days later, 'Don't forget the experiences one has in life as I have had make one hard and persistent ... I don't believe in heaven and hell, but in alive and death.' (21 April 1944)

Dad's musings were evidence of the impact on his state mind of the time spent in internment camps. He frequently refers to being hospitalised.

'I am in the hospital since yesterday with nerves trouble. The main cause are you, my dearest, because we had a rather bad week behind us and I am worried to death about you. What have you done to me that I am ill now? There must be a reason again?'
He can't get through to her (later that night), '... you are too good for a boy like me and that is the reason for denying my love toward you. Can't you understand me, darling?' (17 July 1944)

And then he blames her, *'Still in hospital ... I was already a little wild again and my state worse reading your letters over and over again, you punish me more and more ... my health is suffering. Only one cause and that is your lack of trust in me.'* (18 July 1944)

'... still in hospital ... I'm in the worst temper and rather ill.' (19 July 1944)

They persist with the letter writing, infrequent phone calls and planned dates, possible when Dad can get to Melbourne. Their love does develop despite the obstacles.

'You know I love you with the glorious beat of my heart, and I know that you do, too. Let us stick together and we will find our way.'
(8 September 1945)

By the time the war has ended, they have found a rhythm, are still together, but now I can see that external forces were in play in another way.

'Up to this stage was not so easy, we had to fight and stand up for our love and defend our rights our hearts were asking for ... The future will be harder still and we have to fight for our living and existence.'
(1 August 1946)

And finally, he writes to Mum on the eve of their wedding.

'Well, my Darling, this is the day at last we were looking forward to for such a long time and we thought sometimes it would never happen to us. Now it will happen in a few hours. Just imagine after three and a half years, don't you think it's a miracle after all what happened in those dark and often not promising months? Yes, my sweetest, it will be our day and we will be together for the rest of our lifes.

My gorgeous, this will be my last letter to you because from now on we two live together as one person. What mine is yours and what is yours is mine and we shall solve our problems together and part our sorrows between us.

Darling, for the last time, let me repeat my promise: I shall be yours now and forever. I shall and will trust you in every way, whatever it may occur to us is necessary. I will look after you and keep you as my most valuable treasure and love you more and more until my last day comes in the end and thereafter.

Darling, you know you are the only jewel I have got and I need you desperately, so please stick to me and never let me go or anything happen to me. That's all I ask from you.

We will have to fight hard, but if you take my side of things, it will be much easier for both of us! I realise quite well, my sweetest, that our and especially your life won't be just fun to look after two old people and start a home at the same time, but promise me, darling, that you will take my advice in matters and let me lead the household and be assured that I'll do my best to keep the peace and my surroundings as comfortable as possible.

*Now, my Gold, let me come to the last point. Let me go with you into
heaven for just a little while and let me tell you with kisses and my heart
how much I love you. Sweetheart, I am longing for you and to give you
all I have. I know I am troublesome sometimes but it's only because I
haven't got you all together, but from today on it will be different!*
*So let me close a further step in our lifes, my future wife, and let us be
as happy as we possibly can and start with hearts full of wishes and
hopes for the better or the worst.*
Goodbye the old life, bury it and welcome to the new.
Let me carry you to our paradise and be happy in the ocean of love.
  Always and Forever
  Yours Karl'
(9 December 1947)

It has been a little weird and uncomfortable reading dating love
letters between my parents. Personal feelings and stories from their
early days were never spoken of. Even when I was living through my
first boyfriend disappointments, they didn't share anecdotes to help
me understand my feelings or show me how to cope.

I did pick up a tone of discontent and disapproval of the emerging
liaison from Mum's sister and mother.

*'I couldn't wait to get back upstairs after tea to read your letter again
without eyes on me. I told Ormee and Mother I was writing to Ron,
another fellow from the dance. It's just easier for us both that way.'*
(3 December 1946)

My parents had never talked about it. It was a snippet heard recently
as an anecdote from Lois, the daughter of my aunt's friend. I'd asked
about her early memories and the story was that on the day of my
parents wedding, there were many tears shed by my auntie Ormee and
grandmother Kitty because 'Esmee is going to marry a German.'

How was a baby girl going to crack through this tight unit?

CHAPTER 18

Forever

Dear Chris,

It's January 2017, the first anniversary of living without you. This morning, a simple heartfelt message pinged on my phone. It was Bec:

Those we love don't go away.

They walk beside us every day …

Unseen, unheard, but always near

Still loved, still missed

And very dear.

(From Grave Situation by Alex MacLean on Pinterest)

You'd be impressed at how thoughtful she's been in supporting me, but you believed she and Michael were very special friends, didn't you?

You don't know this though, or maybe you do? Inside my left wrist, I have a tattoo now. In script font, it says simply *forever*. The 'r' has a swish into a heart. Inside is a fine red shadow, but the two halves of the heart don't quite meet. The heart is broken.

Do you remember the night you finally settled on the engraving for the silver bangle, your last birthday present to me?

It was still thirty degrees at 11.00 pm and neither of us could sleep. We pumped up the camping mattress and set it up in the loungeroom so we could take advantage of the cool breeze coming in through the front door. Your pain meds were barely giving you the promised relief and, although we didn't say it out loud, we both knew time was running out. But you still had me laughing so hard my face was aching, especially with the final instructions for your ashes.

'I want Jesus eyes painted on my urn, just like those old paintings of Christ that all good Catholics have in their houses. You know the ones? Where the eyes look like they're following you round the room to make sure you behave.'

'Sure,' I said, 'and who will be the lucky keeper of this urn?'

'I want you to make sure it rotates every six months through houses, starting with Jane's.'

And you went on to name everyone on the list whose apologies hadn't met your strict requirement for a proper heartfelt sorry. You were so sensitive and, to be honest, it was easy to misstep with you. Remember when you were so impressed with Bec's apology that you kept the text to quote it as an example to others!

I know it was your way of easing the tension around your imminent death, so I went with the game, hoping the momentary distraction would help you somehow.

And then you said, 'I've found it!'

'Found what?' I asked.

'The word! Every time you wear the silver bangle, I want you to be reminded that I will be with you in some way, and I will love you, wherever I am,' and then you paused, looked through my eyes into my heart and said, 'forever'.

~

Do you remember the morning you called me and said, 'Hey, Mish, meet me at Café Matto for coffee? I need you to see something.'

And as soon as you walked in, I could see we had a problem.

'You're yellow! The whites of your eyes look like butter!' I said so loudly other diners turned to look. I knew from when I had Hepatitis A years before that it meant there was a liver-related problem.

'Have you made a doctor's appointment?'

'Not yet. I wanted to ask you first,' you said.

That was the way we survived, wasn't it? When either of us had a problem or a decision to make, we'd call the other and work it through together. Did you know Joe described us as being more like a married couple than many married couples? Remember when we went to that speed-dating event as each other's wingmen and potential singles approached at the bar during the break?

'Do you two know each other?'

'Why?'

'You look pretty comfortable together. Sure you're not a couple?'

Giggling like teenagers, we left soon after.

~

You were a unique individual, Christopher A Milne, who could never be described as vanilla. Your vocabulary alone, a result of reading widely and often, was at the upper end of the bell curve.

'I think while I'm in hospital I'll start rereading the classics again,' you announced.

You were in the middle of packing your hospital bag for the seven-hour surgery known as a Whipple. It was named after A O Whipple, a pioneer in modern surgery of the pancreas. His name is now used as an eponym for resection of the head of the pancreas. I knew all about the Whipple from watching the series *Grey's Anatomy* on television, but you were more interested in planning your recovery.

Remember when you nagged me to go to Dr Jo? After years of avoiding dentists, I was always covering my smile to hide the state of my front teeth. I would've eventually stopped smiling if you hadn't persisted in finding a solution. Even as we drove to the first appointment, you kept reassuring me.

'Jo is calm, and I'm sure she'll understand if you tell her the kitchen table story.'

And you were right. Dr Jo's compassion for my childhood terror was the key and she became my dental angel. Years of avoidance cost me thousands to repair, but it was worth every cent and every anxious hour spent in her chair with uncontrollable, full-body shaking. These days it's less discernible but still happens.

Not only did you help me reclaim my smile, I found other dimensions of myself throughout our years together. I was always so serious, but you persisted until you unearthed a sense of fun I'd never had before. We'd play silly word games, shortening long words, lengthening short ones and competing to add the most adjectives to a phrase for 'em-phar-sis'. Your love of language rubbed off on me. How could it not?

'Mish, listen to this, "May in Ayemenem is a hot brooding month. The days are long and humid. The river shrinks and black crows gorge on bright mangoes in still dust grain trees. Red bananas ripen. Jackfruits burst."' You were rereading one of your favourites *The God of Small Things* by Arundhati Roy. You loved to collect examples of evocative prose and read aloud, rolling the words around your mouth with pleasure.

It wasn't long before you volunteered as my sports coach. Rollerblading, Nordic skiing and cycling.

'What do you mean you can't ride a bike? Every kid has a bike. It's a rite of passage growing up.'

'I was never given a two-wheeler,' I said, feeling mocked and trying not to slip into a sulky mood.

'Okay, I'll teach you. Come on, first-born daughter's bike is here. Let's go to the park, now!'

You were more patient than I expected after having instructions snapped at me in your cross-boss tone when you were helping me with something computer related. Once I'd mastered balance and straight-line peddling basics, we hit the tracks you loved to ride at Westerfolds Park, and at last I understood the exhilaration I'd been missing. My prize for going on hundreds of rides with you came when you decided it was time I progressed from a hybrid to a proper competitive mountain bike. On Christmas morning, it was just the two of us and catdog Kev when I saw a magnificently wrapped gift leaning against the wall behind the Christmas tree.

'Go on, open it!'

'Oh my goodness, how long did this take? You've wrapped every centimetre!' I laughed as Kev and I ripped away the red and white crepe streamers patiently twisted around each wheel spoke.

No one had ever done anything as personal, kind and generous as this for me before.

Long before we read the book *Reinventing Your Life* and learnt about schemas, you'd disclosed to me stories of your childhood trauma and I could hear your ongoing argument with the past play out with friends and family. I'd listen for hours while you dissected conversations with Jane phrase by phrase, trying to understand her behaviour and then your own response. You showed me notes after sessions with the psychologist.

'My response when people don't behave and I believe they should: I can become harsh, a bit personal, sometimes sarcastic, more demanding, can turn up the volume—figuratively and actually.'

We both knew that I knew because I'd lived it. Remember the spray you gave me in Berlin?

~

'Quick, Mish, which turn? Come on, can't you even read a map? It's navigation 101!'

'Hang on, go straight ahead. No, wait … I think take the second exit at the roundabout.'

'Not good enough. Now we've missed it!' you shouted.

You shut me down and within a few seconds I was the kid taught not to speak or ask questions, not an adult trying to read a map. We drove on in silence and by the time we reached the hotel you were tired and irritable. I was still smarting, my back teeth clenched with imaginary superglue, unable to get my mouth to form words.

Later, after an awkward dinner, I asked you how you were feeling.

'Mish, I have cancer. How do you think I'm feeling?'

'Wow, you're playing the cancer card! I'm not stupid.'

Now I was the one yelling. You just kept glaring at me, saying nothing, letting the ice cut straight through me.

'Are you seriously saying I'm stupid?'

'Yes, that's exactly what I'm saying. Of course, I'm more intelligent than you,' you fired back.

I was struck dumb. What about all our conversations, sharing ideas and opinions? I'd assumed we both believed we were on an equal footing. Now I felt ashamed and invisible. I might as well have been walking alone on a dangerous road alone at midnight.

When we arrived back in Melbourne a few days later, you said, 'I don't want you here. I can look after myself, Mish.' In your own messed up way, you were trying to protect me from what was coming.

'That's ridiculous, Chrisy. You can't and I'm not going anywhere. I'm very sorry I reacted the way I did in Berlin. I should have been more patient and understanding.'

And again, I found the path back to you by compromising and deferring to you, so our friendship could survive. Despite everything, we remained inseparable, both striving to understand our own wounds and drivers.

You loved quotes and I've kept the journal where you listed them. How often did you quote Socrates?

'The unexamined life is not worth living.'

~

When you were diagnosed with malignant cancer cells, you chose me to walk beside you. On every hospital and medical form you filled out, you listed me as next of kin. I didn't believe I had a choice. Around 9.00 pm, after your Whipple, oblivious to visiting rules, I found a way into the recovery ward to see you. You were spaced out on painkillers so probably don't remember. Lucky for me, the nursing team sensed my determination and let me sit with you until you dozed off again. Seeing you were in brilliant hands, I felt I could leave.

We grew even closer together as we tried to map a way through the unknown future. In the weeks after surgery, there were times when you rang me well before 5.00 am.

'Mish, can you come? Please, now. I can't cope with this pain. It's fucking unbearable. I'm dying, I need you,' you pleaded.

I'd never heard this desperation in your voice before. I threw clothes on, sped to the hospital, mustering enough courage to convince the faces on the other side to unlock the doors and let me into the ward. You needed an advocate. It was my job to make the night nurse understand that waiting for the doctors to do their rounds at 8:30 am wasn't an option. You needed relief right now!

The oncology team at the ONJ Wellness Centre looked forward to seeing you for your treatment sessions. You rarely complained of side effects, remembered their names and always asked how they were. Because you believed you were in the best hands, you accepted chemotherapy as another step to be managed. We took the best pastries in for the team on what we thought was your last infusion. It wasn't a healing miracle, though, was it? It was two years of promise, treatment, scan, anticipation, disappointment, and repeat.

I remember your final appointment with the oncologist. It was a warm day. We went knowing he had the results of the latest scan.

'Chris, there's no more I can do for you. I'm handing you over to the Banksia Palliative Care team.'

And that was it. No formalities, no platitudes, nothing but a card with contact details. We drove home in silence. Made a cup of tea.

'I'm not going to hospital, Mish.'

'What do you mean? The onc didn't say anything about hospital,' I offered.

'I don't want to die in hospital or a hospice. I want to stay here, with you and Kev … please.'

Your face was grey and strained, the nerve at your jawline visibly pulsing.

'Don't worry, Chrisy, you're not going anywhere.'

At no time from when this dreadful thing started did you ask for a timeline. And this day was no different. Did you want to know? It soon hit me. You needed nursing care twenty-four-seven. Could I do it? I'd had no training for this. As your appetite continued to diminish, we'd try anything to make food palatable. It was 1.00 am the night you woke me with a request.

'Mish, I feel like fresh green beans steamed with butter and black pepper!'

While I prepared it, you and catdog Kev set the dining table, including lighting the candles. Despite the time and our pyjamas, we were going to do this in style. We clinked forks, you tried to eat, then you said, 'Sorry, Mish, I'm done.'

It was the last time we sat at that table.

You trusted me completely and despite the self-doubt that had blocked me from so much over the years, as you declined, I grew stronger … for you.

'Mish, am I going to die tonight?'

You grabbed my arm, desperate for connection and solace. Again, I felt your fearful panic.

'No, not tonight, Chrisy, it's not your time yet,' I said, praying I was right.

I had no idea what your dying would mean. When it came, I didn't really understand that you were never coming back. Even throughout those last months, I didn't fully digest the finality of it. After your last breath, I went onto autopilot, doing everything needed to wrap up your life in a way you'd approve of. But you'd gone and I couldn't ask you and it was heart-breaking.

You and I had been inseparable. You'd heard and understood me, and you'd offered me a sense of belonging. You were my family. One of your favourite sayings was *'There is only one thing more painful than learning from experience and that is NOT learning from experience.'* Thank you for giving me the experience.

~

Twelve months have passed since you slipped away. Your absence touches me every single day. There have been so many decisions to make, and I'd relied on you in those times for sixteen years. Now all I can do is talk to your photo. I'm alone, not coping well at all. But if I look at my wrist, I know you're still with me, and will be, *forever.*

Love you, miss you,

Mish xxx

PS: Bec has just texted me again:

'It's hard to forget someone who gave you so much to remember.'

CHAPTER 19

Family Tree

It's 2017, later in the year. I welcome the return of summer and its warmth as the seasons change again. It brings the promise of the expected, wrapped in the hope of possibility. Moving out of Melbourne to Mornington, a beach township, has rewarded me in many ways already. I can walk every day on the sand, along a shoreline of lapping wavelets and finally, I can breathe. I can really breathe.

Packing to move is one thing. Packing up Chris's home only twelve months before was made unnecessarily complex by the competing interests of key individuals. Even that I could have managed. But standing alone in one room and then another, picking up each item of someone's life story and deciding its future, was arduous. Sentimentality and practicality were constantly in play. As I moved between rooms, I moved between states of grief and capability, until I closed the front door for the final time.

Packing up my house was complex in a different way. It required me to make the decisions I had not made twenty-three years before at Ponsonby, the family home. Not only had the stored boxes of secrets come with me, but so had many cherished items of my mother's life story. Furniture, porcelain, paintings. She had loved each item, and I couldn't let them go then.

It took many discussions with Sarah before I could shift the guilt needed to shift the tangible load of prior generations. This was the time for me to stop holding on to the remains of the past. If I was to repair, these reminders could not and would not be coming with me. The recipients were charity shops, second-hand dealers and nosey neighbours taking from the garage sale.

Unpacking is another story, though. I've been methodical. Kitchen, my office, bathroom and bedroom were necessities requiring only the uncomplicated side of setting up a new environment. Having shed the weight of the choices of others, I'm feeling lighter and more playful in this task. Anything that isn't part of my day-to-day needs was put aside to be housed later.

Today is bright, gently warm and I've been feeling more positive by the day. My new office layout offers me an elevated view through double glass doors out to a deck. Without moving from my desk chair, I look up over the top of the Mac and within my line of vision is a foreground of treetops pointing up to the bluest of skies. The neighbour's massive elm is the brightest of grassy green new growth, and the top branches of a ten-metre olive provide a screen to the deck rail. Beyond, to the left, the foliage of indigenous trees moves with the activity of the hidden bird life. I want to be out there enjoying this.

To justify taking a break, I drag out one of the unpacked tubs to sort through. I'd stacked files in here, thinking they were old handwritten client notes needing to be kept but not used. This is a good opportunity to soak up late spring rays while I put some order to my filing system.

I'm making good progress. The next manilla folder is unnamed and unlike others in the pile. It's housing a business-size envelope addressed to me from Judith, daughter of Dad's cousin Hilde who lived in Sydney. I can't recall receiving it, but I must have, as it's been opened. Reaching in, I pull out a wad of half a dozen printed copies of emails dating back to September 2006. They're from a hotmail account.

The name at the top of the page is Klaus Scheye.

I only have to read the first line before my memory jerks the curtain back. Klaus lived in New York and was a cousin of Judith's mother, Hilde. He must have been replying to a question from her as the message begins with an abrupt tone.

Subject Line: Re: Benjamin Family.

'Easy: Karl Heinz' mother was born a Scheye, sister of my father. Both Scheibners died in some camp during World War II. Before they were deported, they left their family papers with my stepmother, Ruth Hoffman, who gave them to me. I forwarded them to Karl Heinz. He acknowledged receipt.

(So, my father had known the fate of his parents!)

The papers showed that his father, a Hungarian-born architect, a government Oberbuerbemeister, was born of Jewish parents but converted to the Catholic faith when young and married my aunt who was secretly converted shortly before her marriage, which must have been a civil one. **Nobody ever knew of this conversion.**

(The foundation of the secret firmly established.)

Karl Heinz was about five years older than yours truly. My father helped him immigrate to the US, but on arrival he was immediately taken to Ellis Island and then deported back to Germany. It seems that on board ship, he claimed to be a Nazi youth member and made it clear that he was not a Jewish refugee.

(This cannot be right! Or is it the truth? Are these the lengths he went to for freedom? I understand why I buried this memory.)

Hilde and my father made it possible for him to immigrate to Australia where he again distanced himself from any Jewish connection. Upon outbreak of the war, he was interned for several years, I recall for the duration of the war. Hilde kept in touch and through her, I was able to send him his family papers.

Hope this somewhat sad tale is not upsetting to his daughter. It is up to you whether you want to transit the details at all.'

Of course it's upsetting for his daughter! What if Klaus is right? How can I possibly share this information with anyone? My father, a member of Nazi Youth?

Then a second email to Judith from Klaus, dated a week later.

I'm compelled to keep reading, knowing I must have seen these communications before but having no recollection. How much of this did my mother know? I feel like I'm now complicit in hiding a pact of secrets.

Subject Line: Scheibner.

'Hi Judith,

I shall try to guess at the true tragedy you may have uncovered. Father and son Scheibner were deeply wounded by the Hitler laws making them both hundred per cent Jews, both having fully Jewish parents. I recall Karl Heinz was enrolled in the Hitler youth organisation at one point.

When Karl Heinz finally started a family and began to settle down in Melbourne, he may have told his family some tale about his background that included by then the Christian Benjamin family of Brisbane which were indeed from the same (Jewish) Benjamin family. Of course, we will never know, but the reputation of the father-son team and fate of Karl Heinz in the USA and Australia seems to support my theory.

The father's occupation was architect and he built post offices and court houses for the Prussian government. It is to build such a government building that he showed up in Lobsens and fell in love with, I believe, Elly Scheye. She became the unhappy and frustrated wife I remember as my aunt, who was not permitted to do more than appear pretty and ladylike.

They did show up for family occasions in the Fink and Scheye house. After all, she was a sister of your grandmother and of my father. The secret of her conversion only became evident when Ruth studied her family papers where it was all spelled out. Karl Heinz was barely polite as he acknowledged receipt of these papers.'

I drop the printouts back into the tub. It's time for a cup of tea and a break. My father wasn't effusive by anyone's definition, but this history of secondary sources paints him as cold and calculating.

And by all accounts, I'm so like my father! Can this be true?

Drinking jasmine tea and staring out to my quiet treed haven, images of my father flash through my mind. None of them recall him as a youthful, cheery, warm Dad. No. My memories begin with the tension at family dinners when he and my aunt, Mum's sister, would snipe until an argument erupted. Thinking back now, I wonder what was at the heart of their constant cold undercurrent?

Having come this far with history I go back to finish the task by reading a third email.

Subject Line: RE: Benjamin family / Scheye

'I am guessing that Karl Heinz was around seventeen to nineteen when he first tried America, and in that span when he got to Australia. His parents died in Auschwitz as did my father sometime around 1943, by which time Karl Heinz was in a prisoner of war camp in Australia.

Memory is a funny thing. I learned under stimulus you recall more. Who knows what else I might dredge up.'

In March 2007, Klaus wrote directly to me.

Subject Line: Carl Heinz

'Welcome to the family; we are a very small family and Walter and I the only survivors, thanks to the events created by history and Hitler. I feel I was extremely lucky to be living to eighty-four and leaving a family behind that seems to be doing well.

Your father was unfortunate, mainly because of the set of parents he picked who sincerely believed that they wanted to leave everything Jewish behind in 1914, but would never succeed in shedding the several thousand-year past. They imparted this sense of leaving the Jewish past to your father, who, as a result, ended up on Ellis Island not being admitted as an immigrant to the US and also as a prisoner of war in Australia.

It was my sad duty to transmit your father's family documents to him only because your grandparents entrusted them to my stepmother who kept them during the war years in Berlin. As I received an acknowledgement from your father, I assume these documents are in your possession. It may be worthwhile to have somebody translate them for you. Why else would your grandparents deliver them to my stepmother within the wake of their deportation to a concentration camp and death?

Your desire to understand this past is understandable and I am certainly prepared to help you with questions you may have. Please understand that I left in 1939, age sixteen, and my memory has gaps. I have no documents relating to the Scheibner branch in my files.

At this point, my main memory is that your grandparents and your father were at every Jewish family festivity, including, I am sure, my bar mitzvah. Your father and I were always expected to play together, stay out of the adults' way. Your grandmother always seemed to be right there ... just in case.'

They were at every Jewish family event, but never revealed the truth of their conversion.

This is not the morning I was expecting. One question after another comes at me. I need to walk it out. I can't talk it out, because the person to do that with is no longer on the end of a phone. It's one of those moments when the absence of Chris as my 'person' hits like a heart punch. So, I walk and walk and walk.

Did I show these emails to Chris ten years ago? Or was I too ashamed? Surely, I'd remember? I must have talked to Judith?

Then a thought kernel emerges. Judith had withheld these emails from me for some time, fearing the tone and content would upset me. She was right. If nothing else, the tone is disparaging and mocking. It does suggest my grandmother Elly was disenfranchised from her family, or at the very least marginalized. What was the impact of this on her? Did she feel isolated? How difficult was it for her to hide her Jewish background? One thing for sure is that my father was reared in an environment of secrets and hidden identities. His life depended on it. Lutheran was his default identity with a very clear message from his mother 'maintain the secret at all cost!'

Back home, at the very bottom of the tub, carefully rolled up in a protected postal tube sent from a New York address, is a copy of the Benjamin/Scheye Family Tree. And there I am.

CHAPTER 20

DNA

It's September 2018, and I've just checked my email inbox for what seems like the hundredth time this week, and it's only Tuesday. Last week was the same, and the week before, and the two weeks before that. Seriously, how long can it take? Making the decision was easier than managing my expectations of the outcome. I haven't told anyone what I've done yet, not even Sarah or Bec. Why not? Part of me, the sensible researcher part, wants proof. I'm fascinated with the work of Dr Rachel Yehuda and her studies on epigenetics, but am I just grasping this concept so that my story has more drama? Is it still this part of me that craves to be heard? I need proof. But why now?

~

One of the many mundane tasks on the list when I moved out of Melbourne down to the beach was to find a new GP. During the first visit, I was reminded again of the sparse detail I had around my family history.

'My father died suddenly at sixty-two with an aortic aneurysm,' I told Doctor Julie. 'As far as I know, his heart had been okay till then. He'd had kidney problems and a bad back, but other than that, I know little else of his or his parents' health status.'

The doctor asked, 'And your mother, any history of heart disease, cancer?'

'Well, her death certificate says cause of death was a brain tumour.

She had been unwell for a number of years with an undiagnosed muscle deteriorating condition. But to my knowledge it was never verified or given a name.'

I described the years my mother spent seeking answers, having test after test, trying everything—including homeopathy—only to get the same answer; the specialists couldn't help her.

'It's been a driver for me to keep fit and maintain muscle strength. I watched her legs waste away first, then her arms, and swallowing had been a problem for years. It became so bad that she could choke on a morsel of food. Then she started having falls around the home and the last one was extremely serious.'

Doctor Julie had been listening whilst tapping away on the keyboard, her eyes on the computer screen. Now she paused and turned to look at me.

'Can you tell me more about what happened?'

'Sure, she was at home on her own, tripped and fell. We think she hit her neck on the corner of a low side-table as she went down. She was able to call an ambulance, and they transported her to the Alfred Hospital. I left work and went straight there, by which time she was admitted to a ward.'

'Do you recall why they admitted her?'

'She had a bad gash on her shin, and they wanted to keep her overnight for observation, thinking she could be concussed. I think they had concerns for her age and mobility due to the obvious limb frailty. As it turned out, it was the right call because later on, the night nurse found her struggling to swallow and breathe. The swelling inside her throat had blocked her windpipe and was so severe the medical team needed to perform an emergency tracheostomy right there and then! If she'd been at home, she likely wouldn't have survived.'

Doctor Julie swung her chair round to face me.

'It would have been a lengthy recovery,' she said.

'Yes, Mum was in hospital for a couple of weeks, and then needed speech therapy to regain the effective use of her voice.'

Later that afternoon, thinking about Mum's ongoing health problems in her final years, I decided it might be time to dig around in Pandora's Box again to see if I had Mum's death certificate. Logic told me I must

have seen it at the time of her death, but what had I done with it? I'd
been so fixated on my father's documents and finding Grant that it had
never occurred to me to question anything in Mum's history.

It didn't take me long to pull out a long narrow yellow envelope, the
sort typically used for legal documents. Inside was a copy of Mum's
will and her death certificate. Reading it did not feel familiar. In fact,
it felt like the first time, but how could that possibly be? A bit over
halfway down the page in section five on medical I found it.

Cause of Death: Right parietal brain tumour – weeks.

Duration of last illness: Severe Myositis – years.

Myositis! I belted upstairs to my laptop and googled it: *a disease
that makes your immune system attack your muscles. It's part of a rare
group of diseases characterized by inflamed muscles, which can cause
prolonged muscle fatigue and weakness.*

She'd known for years that it had a name and she'd never told me.
And I'd been trained and had become an expert at not hearing, seeing
or remembering. Had I also buried this diagnosis from the time I first
received her death certificate in 1994 until now?

Somewhere inside myself, under many layers of guilt and regret, I
felt a question returning to the top. Should I be concerned about this?
Is myositis hereditary?

I'd had enough of Dr Google for one day and grabbed the remote to
distract myself with TV, walking away while it warmed up. From the
kitchen, I could hear the announcer introducing, 'tonight's episode of
SBS Insight Program is DNA Surprises. We talk to people who got
more than they bargained for from a DNA test …'

Grabbing a pen and my journal, I raced back to the loungeroom.
This I had to see.

'Hello and thank you for joining us as we take a look at what happens
when you discover a family secret about your DNA.'

The premise of the program was that investigating our ancestry
can help us connect with relatives and explore our heritage. For many
guests in the audience, and those on the panel telling their stories,
they'd discovered more than they bargained for. It was a collection
of people revealing unknown accounts of parentage and subsequent
cultural backgrounds, including previously undisclosed biological

parents. Most guests said they took the test to better understand their ethnicity, like Kim who thought her grandmother 'had some Māori' in her and wanted to know how much. She discovered there was zero per cent. There was a story here!

Then Rose was introduced. All her life she believed she was of Italian background and had lived her cultural Italian identity, even decorating her home with appropriate bunting and garlands. Her granddaughter wanted to know 'how Italian they were' and asked Rose to take the test. Unlike her brother, who also tested, Rose was zero per cent Italian. And so began her search for answers.

I found it all fascinating. What had begun with me thinking a DNA test could fill the gaps in my medical history had now become a quest with much more at stake. Maybe a DNA test could tell me that what I'd discovered of Dad's story was valid, that the blood pumping through my veins also included a different culture to the one I was raised in and was so familiar with. I needed to know that I wasn't making it up. I wanted the answer to 'who am I?'

The next day, I jumped on to Ancestory.com. The home page stated you could find an *Ethnicity Estimate: Discover the places, history and culture that shaped who you are using just your DNA*. I ordered and paid for a test to be sent.

Waiting for it to arrive, I remembered my father's constant state of fatigue. He'd slump into an armchair at the end of the day with a huge sigh, audible right through the house. It was like he had been in battle with every day of life. Since I'd lost Chris, I'd hear that same sigh emanate from me. These feelings of unexplained sadness that I'd carried since childhood had smashed into recent raw and sad events. The DNA test offered the possibility of finding scientific evidence of my history.

I was still agitated about Mum not disclosing myositis, so I went back to Dr Google and typed in 'myositis + hereditary'.

The result from John Hopkins Medicine tells me more.

'Has no known causes. It has an autoimmune component which means the body attacks itself. However, other factors could be a play, and it's still unknown what triggers it. Hereditary inclusion body myopathy can be linked to genetic factors.'

Oh my goodness, what do I do with this? I better make sure Doctor Julie updates my file next time I see her and hopefully she'll be able to tell me more.

The pack arrived within a few days. I slowly took each component out of the padded sealed bag and read the instructions carefully. Then I spat into the tube, secured the top, placed it back in the moulded sleeve and went to the post office.

~

If I check my email once more and there's still nothing from Ancestry.com, I'm going to start digging for the customer service number. I wait for my laptop to wake up before moving the cursor to the Office icon. Click and bingo!

Subject Line: Michelle, your DNA results are in!
I hold my breath. What will I do? My heart races. Once I open that file, I can't turn back. 'Oy vey, just open it already,' I hear from an invisible space behind me.
And there it was … in bold, uppercase, large font.
50% EUROPEAN JEW (Ashkenazi Jews in Central Europe)
I clicked on the button for *Full Results, plus.*
6% Germanic Europe
34% English and Northwestern Europe
7% Scotland
3% Danish and Swedish

Proof that a whole slice of cultural heritage was missing from my identity. In fact, it had been deliberately denied to me. Feeling elated, I began searching the site, looking for matches from within the Ancestry.com database of possible relatives.

Wait till I tell Sarah about this!

Part Two

Evolving

*"The story you're telling doesn't start on page one.
It started long before you got there."*

Lisa Cron, Story Genius

CHAPTER 21

Disconnected

It's 2017, a Sunday night much like any other. Another weekend has evaporated, another one where I've felt invisible. I'm watching a documentary about a *'woman whose life has been a dance around her family's secrets, their traumas echoing in her choices and in her soul's faded cries,'* the TV guide says.

The first scene unfolds with sweeping views of a coast, hinting at a sense of isolation. The camera zooms in and we see the woman walking, head down, wearing sunglasses and a cap. The voiceover tells us, 'I'm deliberately taking an unfamiliar path so I can avoid meeting familiar faces. It's a ritual I can't fully explain, but it's become a safe zone from the expected line of questioning.' The camera follows her. Then we hear a barrage of invisible voices asking, 'How was your weekend? What did you do? Anything exciting?'

In the next scene, we see her talking to a therapist who asks her why she prefers to walk alone.

'Who wants to be the person who answers, "I did nothing. I stayed in bed with a romance novel because I couldn't bring myself to catch up with friends telling me about their wonderful family holidays and hugely successful businesses?"' she responds. 'I'd rather just pass through the streets incognito, listening to ballads on Spotify, than have to explain anything to anyone.'

Then she adds, 'They wouldn't understand.'

I sense the weight of envy inside her complaints. It's familiar and my body leans toward the screen as a sign of recognition and support. She recalls moments spent with a particular friend who has the uncanny ability to cut through the veneer with a simple question, 'How are you *really*?' That one word, 'really', holding the power to expose her concealed feelings and the thoughts driving them.

'I can't *really* explain it!' the woman says.

The screen goes black.

Then the pace and style changes and the narrator introduces Judith E Glaser, author of the book *'Conversational Intelligence (C-IQ)'* and creator of a training program for leadership coaches by the same name. She tells the camera that her approach is rooted in the neuroscience of conversation.

'When we know what they know, then we're like that person, and our brain loves it. I have a very juicy chemistry when I start to be like you and feel like we have a lot of connection. Trust comes from that feeling. The woman we just watched walked alone because she didn't feel connected to the people in her world and couldn't trust them with her truth.'

This is enough for me to hit pause, grab my phone and start researching Judith E Glaser. I learn that she's a highly accomplished and credentialled organisational anthropologist who has studied and researched in various academic fields, including human behaviour and development, psychology, anthropology, linguistics, neuroscience and transformational social sciences. I need to get my teeth into something with intellectual substance that will engage my mind for at least part of each day and give me a renewed energy in my business. A bonus will be the relief from the empty absence of Chris. I decide to enrol in her accreditation program.

~

The C-IQ training is online and within the first month, I've learnt so much about the profound impact of social isolation. Dr Matthew Lieberman is one of the social neuroscientists who now believe that our need to belong trumps our need for safety. In his YouTube talk on *'Social Pain'*, Dr Lieberman says our need for social connection is as primal as our need for food and shelter and that the absence of it, such as rejection or isolation, can manifest as a form of physical pain.

I wonder if that woman in the documentary had been rejected in relationships. Maybe a lover who couldn't commit? Maybe a family who she feels disconnected from? Dr Lieberman says that we are born unable to care for ourselves, only surviving infancy because someone responds to our cries. Babies cry not just for hunger, thirst, or cold; they cry when separated from caregivers because social separation causes them pain. He uses brain imaging studies to demonstrate that the brain regions activated during physical pain also light up in response to social pain, showing the overlap between the two. Dr Lieberman says these situations of prolonged rejection can lead to depression and other health issues. Leaving it untreated can erode self-worth and impact self-perception. *And self-identity,* I say out loud to the laptop screen. *I wonder if my weekends of intentional solitude are a form of depression.* I must ask Sarah.

One of the assignments for this course is to keep a weekly journal of observations of our own behaviours, 'as well as those we see when we observe our clients in the workplace.' In my journal, I ask myself this question: *Do I choose solitude as a form of protection?*

I begin writing whatever comes into my head without editing or censoring.

Yes, I think so. It works to shield me from the shame of unmet social expectations of marriage and parenthood. It gives me space to daydream about a different life, a normal life as an adored partner and a loved mother. I'm constantly watching my language so I don't reveal my singledom. I'm too ashamed to say that out loud. It's tiring being on alert like this. Is this how Dad felt? Was he worn out from concealing secrets and the burden of unspoken stories? Did Mum respond to my cries, or was she too busy with Daphne? I'm not depressed. I'm sad, all the time, and I cry a lot, but isn't that normal when people leave you? When Dr L talks about social pain, does that include grief? I think Mum was consumed with grief and it ate away her physical strength. Am I in danger of the same happening to me if I continue to exile myself?

Reading this back afterwards, I'm shocked at who I've become. How did I get here?

The next session in the online course is a Q&A with Judith Glaser on social pain. She replays the clip where Dr Lieberman suggests that recognising the importance of social connections, understanding it deeply within ourselves, is crucial because it is our most powerful asset for well-being—even more powerful than wealth. Someone has put in the course chat that they're still connected to school friends and how great it is to have a common anchor. Ha! When I left school, I was happy to leave it all behind. I wasn't connected to any friendship group strongly enough and the final slap was when I was nominated for General School Colours until a hidden face deemed me unsuitable. Connection to me means shared interests and values, empathy, understanding and a desire to support.

Why am I still thinking about school? It was last century!

In my journal that day, I start with a question: *Who did I feel most connected to during secondary school?*

There was Virginia and also Jacqui. They both had two sisters at the school, of similar ages with matching names. Most of the other girls were a same-but-different version of each other. Except Robyn Beckmann. She was an only child. They were Jewish and I loved spending time at her place. We'd walk there after school and pick flowers along the way. Then we'd press them between blotting paper to dry out and we'd use them to decorate gift cards. In Form Three, I stayed over on a Friday and went to Hebrew class with her the next day. It was strange and cool at the same time. Not long after that, she was sick and didn't come to school for a week or so. I wrote her a letter saying I missed her and loved her and included some pressed flowers. It was a symbol of innocent affection for a friend. A few days later, I was called to the principal. Mum was there listening as I was suspended for a week for encouraging a lesbian relationship. What! Are you kidding? Do not talk about this with anyone and that includes Robyn, they said. You are not to speak to her again. Mum didn't utter one word to me on the way home and I got the silent treatment for the next week. I complied out of shame and never mentioned it again. My friendship with Robyn vanished. I was always on the outer ring of the friendship group after that. Connected but not really. Was it painful? It stung.

Reading this back, I feel heartbroken for those two young girls who had their caring friendship stamped on. I just wanted to connect with and understand how this other family lived.

The missed opportunity still stings.

I go back to the notes I took for the module, in particular, Judith's examples of the interplay of neurochemistry between oxytocin, the bonding hormone, and cortisol, released when we're stressed. She gives us a 'Neuro-tip' for each module, and I print out the slide for this one. It says our brains are designed to be social. The need to belong is more powerful than the need for safety. When we feel rejected, it activates our fear networks and increases the levels of cortisol, which moves us into protect behaviour. *'Focus on inclusion and appreciation to reduce the level of cortisol and increase oxytocin.'*

I've also underlined, *'oxytocin plays a significant role in building and strengthening trust and connection. When we have open, honest and empathetic conversations, our oxytocin levels rise. Cortisol triggered by stress and anxiety can lead to a defensive need to withhold information and mistrust others.'*

The demeanour of the woman in the TV doco persists in my mind as I revise this module. She doesn't give us intimate details of her life, but it's clear to me she carries a burden. Her expression at the start was intimidating, and then she began to mellow with understanding. I've been described as intimidating, most likely learnt from years in the classroom. Defensive? No doubt. Anxious? Often.

After rereading, I add a note in red pen in the margin of the notebook next to where I've written *'cortisol can cause your body to freeze up and you can't find the words to respond (Berlin and Chris, and every time I'm asked if I have children).'* Judith has given us a one-pager of behaviours to do and say more of and less of.

Now I highlight and circle, *'distrust comes from keeping secrets and not sharing; trust builds when we reveal more and tell the truth.'*

CHAPTER 22

Metaphorical

It's 2019 and I'm consumed with self-blame over the imminent tanking of another relationship. I couldn't sleep last night until well after 4.00 am. *Why do I keep attracting prospective partners who can't commit? I wrote in my journal. Why am I so compliant? Why do I get snarky when I sense Phil's withholding something from me? And why do I shut down when I feel threatened?*

I've been asking myself these questions for decades. Nothing new to see here. Have I forgotten everything I've been learning for the past six months? Perhaps I'm being too hard on myself, again. Since moving to Mornington, I've consciously planned strategies to help me settle into this new community. I joined a local business group and despite how hard I find it initiating chat with strangers I showed up at the first event not knowing one other person. I made an intentional effort to get out socially. How else was I going to bump into a potential partner? Then I joined Dine Date Love, a dinner-for-six group based on the Mornington Peninsula for singles to meet safely over dinner. And I met Phil.

~

Moving away from the familiarity of the neighbourhood where I taught for all those years whilst learning about infidelity; where my home haven was tarnished with memories of Matthew's uninvited exchanges that left me bruised and shaken; where Chris's truncated future was announced; where every reason to move was a decision wrapped in the optimism of a healthier and happier future, was momentous. Relocating hasn't silenced the old questions from new acquaintances. 'What are you doing for Mother's Day?' still slices through me, and has done annually since Mum passed away. Or going to dinner for six, and being at a table with five parents who begin their conversations with, 'How many children do you have?' Meanwhile, I continue to ask myself in my journal, *Where do I attach myself now? Where do I belong now that I'm no longer a daughter, never been a mother, not a partner, etc.? Where do I fit in this new location? Is there a valid label I can use to make it easier for people to accept my differences?*

I've come to recognise that I collect knowledge like a librarian collects new books. However I stay captivated until something new presents itself and then I move on before I've digested each learning. Surely by now I should be managing myself with more poise and patience. I need to pause, breathe deeply and appreciate every volume I have before moving on.

It's a good time to weigh up what I have so far. Chris and I discovered 'lifetraps' in Jeffrey E Young's book *'Reinventing Your Life'*. Young wrote about recurring patterns that need our deeper consideration to see how negative thinking and behaviour often stem from early life experiences. I had always thought my childhood life was normal. But I can't remember simple things like Mum's perfume, or resting happily on her lap while she read to me, or hanging out with Dad in the garden hearing about 'when he was my age'. Is lack of physical nurturing neglect? I can recall sobbing with fear every time I was taken to the doctor, dentist or town hall for injections. 'The sooner we get in the sooner we're out' was the standard aside. Young wrote that neglect and trauma can shape our core beliefs and self-perceptions. Were my anxiety attacks an involuntary reaction to anaesthesia by ether on the kitchen table? By naming these fleeting examples, am I recognising, understanding and naming my lifetraps of Abandonment and Emotional Deprivation? Now can I work on breaking free from their grip? I'd followed his advice to seek out professional help to challenge my negative thought patterns and develop self-compassion. Since finding Sarah, I've worked on identifying the turmoil my mother would have been in with a newborn baby. She must have been still grieving the absence of Grant, caring for Auntie Daphne's every need, and supporting Dad. Did this draw her focus away from me, an apparently healthy, easy baby? She must have suppressed her own needs, leaving minimal emotional bandwidth for me. Young wrote that this dynamic often leads children to grow up seeking validation as they struggle to accept their worth. I now wonder if that's what I've been doing as I repeatedly seek external endorsement, both professionally and romantically.

Two years ago, the Universe had delivered me Judith Glaser's pioneering work in the neurochemistry of conversations. She explained the significance of fostering oxytocin, the bonding hormone, as the key to building trust and more meaningful connections. Glaser had also shown me how cortisol, the 'stress' hormone, can contribute to weight gain. Hello! I grew up managing my weight, just like Mum did. When I was with Greg, my weight ballooned to 82 kgs and it took hard work to get back to a healthy range. I've been on the same roller coaster ever since, especially in the aftermath of losing Chris. I had talked this through with Sarah and understood now that Dad had experienced social isolation and high anxiety levels most of his life, evident in the emails with the subtext of disapproval from Klaus.

Sarah introduced me to the idea of the internal family systems model, which encouraged me to look at the different versions of my inner self. When I first entered her rooms, I was still wearing the face of Professional Michelle. But now I can see there is another version of me, a young Michelle who repeatedly worries that *I can't remember anything else about those times.* This still bothers me deeply, and I have an internal imposter who has been present and demanding. *Who am I to be telling Sarah details of my life that I have no proof of?* I've also uncovered my loner self, the part of me who has been content to spend hours alone feeling the sadness of grieving before I even knew what grief was. There must be reasons for this, but try as I might, I can't access the memories. On the other hand, some things have stayed in my mind on repeat, like *you look more like your father than your mother.* Why is that so clear and important to remember? Will I ever understand it?

~

By the time I happened upon David Drake and his theory of 'narrative coaching', I was already aware of the impact of so-called 'personal narratives' on our perceptions, choices and emotions. I'd encountered these ideas when I did the Landmark Forum, my first large group personal-development experience. It was during the time Matthew had moved out but persisted in staying attached through regular contact that I was incapable of shutting down. The Landmark Forum promised the *'secret to powerful life transformation'* by *'breaking free of victimhood and confronting limiting beliefs.'*

We were given various tasks over the three days, all designed to shake us up. Day One began with an exercise to write about the one thing about ourselves we wanted to change. I wrote about feeling unworthy of marriage. The way I described my relationships with Greg, Matthew and Simon, it was as if they were awards I'd missed out on through my own flaws.

With our stories in hand, we paired up. Person One was asked to read their story out loud to Person Two who was instructed not to comment or ask questions. Then we swapped. Then we swapped again, still not engaging with the details. This continued with each pair having several opportunities to read their versions out. Eventually all I could hear of my story was a gaggle of meaningless words, like the kid's song, *Old MacDonald had a farm ee i ee i oh, and on his farm he had some cows, ee i ee i oh with a moo-moo here and a moo-moo there.* We laughed as we heard our own words morph into farmyard racket, and then we saw very clearly that it was just a noisy story we'd been telling ourselves.

But breaking old habits and changing ingrained behaviours requires a compelling driver and The Forum environment wasn't for me.

~

Often when I'm with Sarah, I hear myself getting stuck in the minutia of the story I'm telling, and I'm reminded again of Old McDonald's

Farm. I notice how she brings me back to the feelings provoked, rather than asking more about details. Observing her technique prompts me to consider how I can update and enhance my coaching skills and I remember being impressed with Dr David Drake. I'd watched a single-session immersion called 'How to Release Old Stories and Start Living New Ones' three years ago. As I'm trying to find my notes, the Universe delivers me an email about his next online training course for coaches. Without hesitating, I sign up.

Narrative Coaching is grounded in both academic rigour and Dr David's deep personal understanding of how people change by working at the level of identities. He says that our stories are in every cell of our body and impact us even without us realising it. I like his phrase, *the content of our story is the door into the house, to finding the heart of the roadblock or limiting self-belief.* He says the facts of the story aren't as important as the feelings we experience when we tell the story, and we can use this to bring about transformational change. I keep falling back into the old habit of trying to make the relationship work with Phil even though I can feel his resistance to commitment. Whatever the story is I'm telling, I can't change him. So, I need to change.

~

The first Dine Date Love dinner I went to—the one where I met Phil—was only a few weeks after I'd moved out of Melbourne. I felt confident that my scars were hidden, that I hadn't brought any lingering issues with me. I walked into the Girl & Bull restaurant ready to write a new chapter. Phil and I clicked over a witty exchange as I sat down, and we easily engaged in pacey banter and a relationship was ignited. We were matched in intellect and wit, but this eventually became a stumbling block rather than an asset. We are no longer speaking, and I'm stuck in the same repetitive story of failing to be 'the one'. I'm doing life solo again.

The end began about a year in. One night after dinner, it blew up. My dreams were often set in the wilderness of biblical times and the most recent was still in my mind. In telling Phil, I mentioned my long-time desire to visit Israel and Jordan. The exchange burst into an argument about history, religion and faith. Our listening skills failed us both and I couldn't move past the feeling of not being heard, and all he could hear from me was the 'coaching' tone of Professional Michelle.

'Don't speak to me like I'm your client,' he tossed back over his shoulder as he walked out of my house, slamming the front door.

And that was it. I had felt the absence of commitment, lack of any future planning and I wondered if Chris's presence around my home may have been a deterrent. I needed to let Phil go.

In the weeks following, I collected evidence of all the times I believed he was being evasive, and I used it to prove to myself that it's a technique he uses to stay detached. I concluded he had a lingering passion for another woman, and I didn't measure up. There was no real proof, just me trying to make sense of why he was keeping me at arm's length. And so there I was, back at the old familiar place of not being enough.

This wasn't the first argument we'd had, but it was the nastiest and it had a finality about it. Chris used to say to me that each person has equity in an argument, so I'm prepared to own my part and try to understand how I can use these new tools I'm learning to change my behaviour in the hope of attracting a new future. I'm committed to following the Narrative Coaching formula to improve outcomes in my work, and I'm also hopeful of changing my own story in the process. In his book *'Narrative Coaching'*, Dr David says we can see the interconnectedness between our realities, our stories and our identities, and the systemic and self-fulfilling prophecies that tend to keep it all in place. *Is this serving a similar purpose to the way we form a lifetrap or schema?* It's clear to me, so far, that our stories about ourselves, what we think is going on and what we think caused it 'including a collective cultural response from preceding generations', have implications for how we make decisions every day.

As Dr David Drake says, our role is to facilitate the formation of new narratives, not fix broken ones. In doing so, he says ask the question, how is your story serving you? Not serving you? What are you afraid will happen if you let that story go? What would a different story help you see or do? But I'm not sure I can let my story go. I need to go back to one of the first tools he gave us about self-regulation.

If I look at what happened in that final argument, my version is that Phil wasn't listening and didn't hear the depth of meaning inside my unexplained desire to visit Israel. What I heard him say was that Israel had nothing to do with feeling Jewish. I assumed he was discounting something very important I'd discovered about my identity. The part of me confirmed by the recent DNA test became invisible in this conversation and so I reacted. I was triggered, and he walked out.

In that moment, the Childlike part of me felt unimportant, stupid and disconnected. What was I telling myself? The Imposter part of me said Phil was showing up my lack of understanding about the state of Israel. What does this say about how I see myself? That I am a stupid imposter and the Survivor said I'm not worthy of genuine love. What did I do as a result? I hid behind Professional Michelle again. What happened in the end? Phil proved me right by leaving.

If I rewind this story, what outcome would I have liked to happen? Phil says, 'What's stopping you? I'll come to Israel with you'. What could I have done differently as a result? I could have encouraged his gesture and accepted that I don't have to do everything alone. What would need to shift in how I see myself? I need to shift from seeing myself as so unworthy that the only person I can rely on is myself. What could I tell myself next time this happens? I've been triggered and so misinterpreted what he said. What would I observe if this were the case? I would have asked for clarification from him to see if he misheard me and together, we could have reset the discussion before it escalated.

It sounds doable, but how can I remember and make it stick? I haven't yet integrated any new versions of my story, so I can't be sure what will happen next time I'm triggered. I notice that Sarah often uses a metaphor to reinforce a breakthrough I've had in a session with a visual cue, and this does help me remember. Dr David talks about using metaphors to bridge between the old world we want to change and the new perspective of our situation, the new story we tell ourselves.

I go back and rewatch the section in the module where he says metaphors offer hints about issues the person has yet to find language for. When he asked, 'Are you more like a sketchbook or a blueprint?',

I immediately wrote down 'sketchbook' because it's the way I like to think and work. I've been using an A3 size sketchpad to plan my speaking content, by brainstorming and mind mapping concepts and keynote ideas. It helps me visualise the links and themes from all the sources I've absorbed over years of reading, learning and coaching. It's time I grab my coloured pens to create a visual representation with simple drawings of my internal parts. I start with Detached Michelle, alone and lonely, self-protecting in the upper corner of the page. Then I add Childless Michelle with empty eyes, and a hollow heart, forgotten, feeling like a parental failure. Hiding in the shadow is The Imposter, busy self-sabotaging, always comparing, contrasting then doubting herself. I acknowledge Survivor Michelle who's resilient, strong, courageous and independent by using an orange highlighter to remind me that every sunset has a sunrise. She keeps me afloat, but she's self-protecting, and when she jumps in defensively, it pushes others away.

On the top of the page, I write: *How did we arrive here?*

CHAPTER 23

Jigsaw

April 2020, Anzac Day, dawn, and I'm standing in my driveway holding a flickering candle and listening to The Last Post. The air is crisp, and the sound is chilling. My neighbour, Richard, has set up his sound system so we can hear the service from the Shrine of Remembrance. I sneak a look and see he has hung the Australian flag on his fence post. Rhys, from the house opposite, and his dog, Smokey, are watching from their deck. We all nurse our personal memories and our reasons for getting up so early to do this. When the radio broadcast finishes, we call out a neighbourly farewell before heading in doors. We're in this together, locked down in our homes, staying two and a half metres apart, unable to travel outside a five kilometre radius while the world adjusts to the first global pandemic in one hundred years.

The lockdown decree was initially for two weeks, then it was extended to a month, and now autumn has become winter. Winter is my Achilles heel. Shorter days, grey skies and one anniversary after another, starting with Dad's birthday, followed by Mum's, then the anniversary of her death, with Dad's nine days later and Chris's birthday, all within six weeks. In previous years, Sarah has explained this to me as seasonal affective disorder and this time around it feels intense. I don't see one smiling face when I go for my short, permitted walk, because we're now told to wear masks when exercising outdoors. The people in my business networks are all working from home, doing their best to survive. John and his Perth family aren't locked down. They're able to gather for celebrations and weekends away and I don't know how to feel happy for them.

I'm back to being the brooding isolate I was in 2016, before I found Sarah. The steps forward I'd made working through the Narrative Coaching program with David Drake have been fading during the isolation of lockdown. My sessions with Sarah are now conducted online via Zoom. I'm grateful to have an alternative, but I miss the drive down Hotham Street and her beautiful energy in the room. She's been a safe guide for my journey away from daily episodes of grief.

'How do you feel about lockdown?' she asked recently.

I heard myself recount all the same complaints about how *people don't understand how hard it is to do life on your own.* Even as I was talking, I could hear how ungrateful I sounded.

'Look, being an introvert has helped me adjust, but still, some days I don't see the point of getting out of bed.'

'Is it possible you've done a stellar job of convincing people that you're okay?' Sarah asks, after my twentieth complaint about the radio silence from Perth.

I know what she means. My default pattern, learnt from watching my mother I suspect, is to rely only on myself. That's who I trust, who I know will wake up with me tomorrow.

'I've been calling to check in with past clients, but you can only do that once. I don't want to become a stalker,' I tell her. 'I've thought about putting a post-COVID program together as a roadmap for folks who might be using this time to rethink their career plans, but I'm just not feeling enthusiastic about that either.'

'What would Chris say to you right now?'

'He'd say maybe you need to expand your brain and learn something new.'

I promise Sarah I'll think about it.

~

Now it's March 2021, and we're back in lockdown. I can feel the chill of the approaching winter creeping in again from the Southern Ocean. By now, this time a year ago has been carved into history as the beginning of the politicians' response to the pandemic. For twelve months, I've been noticing the impact of lockdown on myself, on neighbours and on a global scale. I deliberately stay away from conspiracy theories, but there are days when it feels like we're living in a social experiment. My friends who have families are finding it challenging working from home and are missing important milestones and celebrations because of the lockdown restrictions. But I'm going okay and, for the first time, I'm grateful for the part of me who identifies as a survivor. I'm accustomed to living solo and have chosen personal isolation often, making conscious and unconscious decisions to live this way since Dad died.

As we all navigate the confines of our homes, a curious phenomenon has emerged. Looking for a way to pass the time, people have become obsessed with putting together jigsaw puzzles. Being a crossword person, jigsaws have never been an activity I'd think to do. But I'm getting tired of crosswords. Phil works in residential construction which has been deemed an essential service, so his day-to-day working life is still relatively normal. We can't spend time together, but he thought I needed a diversion and dropped off a jigsaw puzzle for me, including a board to lay it on as sections come together. Very thoughtful.

He and I have now moved on from a relationship to a friendship and I appreciate him looking out for me. I resisted his gestures initially, telling myself I didn't need another ex-partner turned friend. But right now, I'm thankful that he's willing to break the government lockdown regulations about visiting friends. I don't share with him my recent fears about mortality. My age renders me especially vulnerable, a message repeated daily by the federal and state Chief Health Officers, and there's a new worm slithering through my mind as I try to sleep. *What if I contract this deadly virus? No one would know. It could be weeks, months even before anyone would find me. Should I pack a case for hospital? Better make sure my house is tidy in case Bec has to prepare it for sale.*

With little else to do today, I return to the 1,000 brightly coloured pieces covering the tabletop. I find it soothing to sort them according to shape, finding edges first, then design intricacy and colour. The scene on the box depicts the swinging sixties, with young men and women laughing and dancing, embodying the spirit of freedom of their times. I wonder if the 2020s will be as transformative? The phone pings with a notification. Thank goodness for Click and Collect. It's a text message from our local bookshop in Mornington.

'Your order for '*It Didn't Start with You*' by Mark Wolynn is ready for collection.'

This book was recommended to my mate, Scotty, by a psychologist he's been working through issues of depression and anxiety with. I was curious about the title, so I went straight to Dr Google and found a YouTube clip of the author telling his own story. He'd been searching for years to resolve a deteriorating medical condition, and the healing came from an unexpected process.

'*We don't come into the world with a clean hard drive,*' he said. '*There is an operating system already in place that contains the fallout that our parents and grandparents experienced.*' This sounds like the conversation I had with Sarah about my dad's experience as a young boy, learning to maintain the silence of his mother's faith conversion, only to repeat the silence himself.

On Mark's website, I find a *List of Family Questions* that he says are clues that one's family history could be the software running life in the background. Seven of these questions are popping like neon signs.

Who was abandoned, isolated, or excluded from the family?

Who was adopted or who gave their child away?

Who experienced a significant trauma or suffered a catastrophic event?

Who suffered in war?

Who died in or participated in the Holocaust or some other genocide?

Who was wrongly accused?

Who was jailed or institutionalized?

Who had a physical, emotional, or mental disability?

In that moment, I know I need to read Mark Wolynn's book. Apologising to the jigsaw, I head out to Farrell's Bookshop, impatient to collect my copy.

~

I have never been that person who uses a highlighter or underlines or writes in the margin of a book. But on page one of Mark's Introduction, my yellow highlighter has found words that feel like they were written specifically for me.

'Even if the person who suffered the original trauma has died, even if his or her story lies submerged in years of silence, fragments of life experience, memory, and body sensation can live on, as if reaching out from the past to find resolution in the mind and bodies of those living in the present.'

The book was published in 2016, the year I lost Chris. I need to understand more about the author. Is this pop psychology, or based on established psychological concepts and family dynamics?

On page two, I learn more about Mark Wolynn. His work integrates the latest findings in neuroscience, epigenetics and the science of language. In the C-IQ program with Judith Glaser and the Narrative Coaching program with Dr David Drake, I'd learnt about neural pathways. Judith constantly reminded us that words can change worlds, so to look more closely at its science is intriguing to me. I was first introduced to Dr Rachel Yehuda, a pioneer in epigenetics and how trauma affects our DNA, in the C-IQ training. We saw then how her research on Holocaust survivors revealed that the legacy of trauma gets passed through generations via molecular imprints and the interplay between the environment and genetic expression. Mark trained with Bert Hellinger, a highly regarded German psychotherapist, remembered for his approach to family therapy. He explained how both the psychological and physical effects of inherited family trauma pass down through generations.

If ever a book was written for me, this is it. The premise is we can unknowingly adopt and keep alive the fears, feelings and behaviours from the cycle of pain of our parents, grandparents and even our great grandparents. In the Introduction, Mark tells us that as a clinician he learnt to listen to language, to the words behind people's complaints and beneath their old stories, revealing the presence of these buried worries and fears. *Just like Old McDonald's Farm*, I say to myself, and already a sense of recognition is awakening inside the empty spaces I live with daily.

~

Packing up the incomplete jigsaw puzzle and carefully piling the sorted pieces into zip-lock bags, I've decided to spend time this afternoon going back over the C-IQ notes alongside Mark's thoughts on epigenetics. My initial reaction is an eagerness to see if Dad's melancholy can be explained by science. When I try to remember specific conversations with him, I have nothing. When Sarah asks me to describe how I knew he was sad, all I can recall is hearing his lamenting and exhausted sigh echoing throughout the house. He was permanently tired, as if life was damn hard, yet in my mind our life was normal. Dad had never shared any tales of Nazi brutality, or antisemitic bullying, or even the journey from Berlin to Melbourne. And yet I *feel* his grief and have done for as long as I have memories.

I decide to use my A3 sketchpad and flick to a fresh page. First, I do a quick line sketch representing an iceberg. I use every bit of real estate on the paper. I draw a red broken line from left to right, approximately one eighth from the top. I label the iceberg peak 'Visible Above the Line' and add *Professional Michelle, coach and facilitator, articulate, composed, confident, capable, fit and healthy, joyful and successful.* Then, just under this red line, I label *Invisible* and add: *single, raised only child, never married, adult orphan, childless, voiceless, family-less.*

Taking a black pencil, I draw a broken line from left to right at the very base. The first thing I write in is *greater than fifty per cent DNA European Ancestry, Epigenetics, Grief.* Using all my journal notes, I add a key to the facing page with dot points.

1. The sperm you developed from were present in your father when he was a foetus in his mother's womb.
2. The father's sperm continues to be susceptible to traumatic imprints almost up to the point when you are conceived.
3. From the earliest moments of life, cellular biology shapes us emotionally, psychologically, and biologically, influencing our trajectory through time.
4. The mother's emotions such as fear, anger, love, hope can biochemically alter the genetic expression of her offspring.
5. Chronic or repetitive emotions like anger and fear can imprint

her child, essentially preparing or programming how the child will adapt in its environment. (Bruce Lipton, pioneering cell biologist)

6. According to Rachel Yehuda, epigenetics changes our biology to prepare us to cope with the traumas that our parents experienced.

I begin to build a mind map, creating layers between the two horizontal dividing lines showing possible links between the feelings I've lived with and where they may have originated from long before I came into the world. I use my intuition to guide the connections and, for the first time, I wonder if the history of my Grand Folks, Elly and Ludwig, up to and including their transportation to the death camp, has filtered down through Dad to me. Did the continual practiced silence of concealing their Jewish heritage begin before Dad was born? What would it have been like for Dad as a kid hiding his Jewish birthright? Were the circumstances that forced his parents to make the decision for him to leave Germany, only for the bullying to continue inside the internment camp here, so traumatic that he dissociated from the memories? His appeal stated he'd had a nervous breakdown at the camp. Was that a form of post-traumatic stress? Does this sit on my DNA?

I draw a connecting line from 'raised only child' to a bubble labelled 'Grant'. Remembering the session when Sarah and I talked about Mum's experience of carrying a second child to term so soon after losing her first born, I feel her sorrow and her heightened anxiety for the health of me, her second baby.

Sitting back and staring at my work, I wonder what have I stumbled across here? Was I biologically prepared to cope with their individual and joint histories in a way that has influenced mine?

Maybe I need to grab some post-it notes as I read Mark's book. If I record the learnings on yellow ones and the family evidence on orange ones, I'll be able to join the jigsaw pieces of my story.

CHAPTER 24

Systems

It's Mother's Day weekend, 2011, and I'm on a plane from Melbourne to Hobart. I tighten the seatbelt for landing and brace myself for this important mission. The Tasmanian connection has always felt important, yet I can't quite name each branch of the family tree to know where I sit. Dipping through the clouds, the airport buildings appear below, and suddenly I feel like a time traveller. I hope that I'll be boarding the return flight with a decision in my luggage.

I can't recall my most recent visit to Tasmania. There are flashes of memory from long ago—the school holiday spent at the shack on Garden Island when I was about fifteen, meeting a boy, thinking it was first love, writing dozens of letters and, back home later, crying for days because I couldn't see him again. I remember the coastal beauty of Coles Bay, the challenge of walking Mt Amos, the pristine waters of Wineglass Bay and I remember hoping Johnno would come back from early fishing with enough trumpeter fish for lunch. At the heart of these images is Mum's cousin, Helen, or Yel, as number-two son, Johnno, liked to call her. She is the anchor.

I've spent the flight immersed in nostalgia for those times with the Clennett family. Helen's daughter, Sally, was my first style icon. After Auntie Daph died, the upstairs attic became a guest bedroom and Sally would stay with us when she came to Melbourne. She was very tall, very tanned and very beautiful, and the scent of Christian Dior's Dioressence would float down the stairs in her shadow. It became my scent of choice. Johnno came to play AFL for the Melbourne Football Club, studied at Monash University and partnered me to my first

University Ball. And it was Helen's son, Timmy, who was a resident at Kew Cottages until he passed away before reaching driving age. The landing jolts me back to the present and I still haven't quite worked out who is related to who. The threads of connection stretch back to my great grandmother, Flora, a figure still veiled in mystery, but I leave the thought on the aircraft and head across the tarmac eager to see Helen.

Helen has reached the age of ninety years and is the sole person I can trust to explain Mum's decision to place Grant in the care of strangers. She is the person most likely to have been a confidant for Mum, given Timmy was at Kew Cottages at the same time as my brother. Can she share with me the missing pages of Grant's story? My first question for her will be, did you know Grant was still alive?

~

My understanding of the hushed energy within the broader family has gone from zero to one hundred over the years of seeing Sarah. It's taken many conversations of gentle reinforcement to shift my feelings of shame to those of regret whenever I talk about Grant. Many of our early family photos show me as a child playing alone in a sand pit, or on the Rosebud beach, or with adults. Were children in institutions ever taken to the beach to play? With other kids or with their adult carers? I do know Grant lived in several state run 'homes' in different suburbs of Melbourne and then intrastate. When his carer, Stuart, said Grant was unable to comprehend family relationships, I took that to mean he had no understanding of the inference of the label 'sister' or 'brother'. In working with Sarah, my grasp of family connection has expanded.

When I'm in session with her, I will often pre-frame a statement with 'my childhood was normal.' She will ask me to clarify, to which I'll repeat a well-worn version.

'There was no traumatic incident, my parents loved me, they didn't divorce, nothing bad happened, I had everything I needed.'

We've had a couple of attempts at role playing conversations between myself and Mum, Dad, Grant, Elly and other family members.

'If your father was here right now, what would you like to say to him? Don't tell me, face the chair and speak to him directly,' and I'm always tongue tied.

I don't want to hear my own voice ask, 'Why did you give Grant away?' Or say, 'Mum, I was very confused when you'd ignore my questions, or when I'd try to talk to you if you were cross with me and you'd just turn away as if you didn't hear or see me.'

It sounds so disrespectful and ungrateful. And then more tears come, a lump rises into my throat from an unfathomable place and we'd close the attempt to connect with the ancestral energy.

~

Helen now lives close to the Derwent River in Sandy Bay, with Johnno not far away. She is beaming as she greets me, and regretfully I wonder why I haven't come here sooner. She has icy white hair and a walking stick, but her vibrancy defies her age, and she has the same grace as my mother, a presence blunted by early heartache yet a determination to accept the challenges destiny gave her. I need to rekindle the relationship before opening potentially difficult doors. It doesn't take long to get up to date with the family news. There are trips and grandchildren to catch up on, not to mention health and real estate moves.

'Now tell me about you,' Helen asks, so I fill her in with more detail about life after Matthew and then meeting Chris.

Eventually, I get to the part where I met April and her interest in genealogy.

'April found Grant. He's alive and living in country Victoria.'

As those words land, I feel relieved at the intersection of release and pain. Helen's expression is neither surprise nor joy, just measured.

'Well, that's unexpected.'

Being aware of the circumstances, I don't want to push her, so I continue with details of April's detective work and, in that context, ask, 'Did you know he was in Kew Cottages when you went there to visit Timmy?'

'Yes, I did, and yes, Es (my mother), came with me. But after Tim died, I don't know how long she continued her visits there.'

Her expression was contemplative, as if trying to remember, so there was no reason to doubt her.

I ask her who else knew.

'I can't be sure, although I think your Auntie Orm went a few times.'

That doesn't surprise me. My aunt liked to insert herself into Mum's life and opinions especially if it could rile my father. My guess is he wouldn't have encouraged these visits.

I ask her next about her story, and Timmy.

'I was too young to understand why Tim lived at Kew,' I say, 'but have always assumed he was Down Syndrome, as well.'

But the truth was something different.

Helen explains that Tim's birth went well. He developed like any other healthy baby until contracting meningitis as a toddler. Meningitis is an infection of the membranes that cover the brain. Within days, his motor and cognitive abilities declined and then came the devastating news that he would never recover. He became totally dependent. As she's recounting those dark days, including the events leading to the decision to place Tim in care, the detective voice in my head is saying *that means Helen did not birth a disabled child. He had a bacterial disease. My assumption of the last fifty years has been wrong!*

Helen's frame appeared smaller, and her voice faded just enough for me to detect that our conversation was opening a bank of memories, so I move onto the plans for the rest of the weekend. We have dinner with Johnno and his partner. Again, I tell the story of April and finding my brother after a lifetime of absence. Johnno is listening intently because it's the first time he's heard any of Grant's story. Eventually, he asks the question, 'Do you think you will go and meet Grant?'

'That's the question I'm hoping to answer this weekend.'

I tell him about my conversation with Grant's carer, Stuart, and the arrival of the photo pack that didn't resonate. I include the warning from Stuart, 'think long and hard and prepare yourself before making the trip'. I also repeat that Grant is inclined to bursts of anger, making it hard for the carers to manage. Stuart had explained that being my brother would have no meaning to Grant as he doesn't understand the notion of familial ties. I repeat his warning.

'So, if you come expecting a family reunion, you will be disappointed by Grant's lack of interest in who you are.'

'I've discussed it with John and Barb, and they say it's up to me.'

Johnno agreed with their sentiment, Helen didn't say anything and I'm still hoping to head home with a clear plan.

~

After Sarah opened up the subject of family systems, and the couple of attempts I made to connect back into the memories failed, I still believed it was worth learning more about. It was another reason the work of Mark Wolynn appealed to me. Of course, what tends to happen when the Universe recognises your mind is expanding through self-directed exploration, it drops in fresh breadcrumbs. That's what happened when a colleague flicked me news of a new release titled, 'Connected Fates, Separate Destinies: Using Family Constellations Therapy to Recover from Inherited Stories and Trauma' by Marine Sélénée. Adding to my anticipation, Marine trained with Mark and also believes family constellations begin with the premise: it did not start with me.

After reading the first pages, I'm hooked.

'We are part of a family system, and events in that system which predate us may have caused us to act in a way that was beyond our conscious control. By going forward liberated from the narratives of inherited traumas and disordered family system dynamics, we get to tell our own authentic story.'

Marine Sélénée's book presents a new insight into the subconscious instinct to save and repair our family system that often shapes our early years. By exploring the pain of the generations before us, we can uncover patterns where unhealed trauma was passed down from family members. In the introduction, she too refers to Bert Hellinger, who founded Family Constellations Therapy in the 1950s. He says whether we know what happened in our family history or not, the cycle of trauma and pain is imprinted through the generations. Marine Sélénée and Mark Wolynn both discovered their pain was tethered to an event in their past, rather than coming from their own experience. I can't help but ask myself if it's possible that every wound I feel, every complaint about what I *don't* have, every unexplained fear keeping me from moving forward, may have come from a previous generation?

Is it possible that I'm carrying Elly's sorrow caused by converting from her Jewish faith and the family's subsequent shunning of her? Did Dad carry the grief in repeating the secret? Did Grant and Auntie Daphne feel the rejection through isolation from the family? If I'd had children, would I have passed on that pain? Is this the missing link?

Marine explains that every family exists in its own network, sharing the same DNA, culture and stories. An invisible thread links all members together through time in the form of internal family memory. *But what if the stories I've been telling myself are all wrong? Based on the wrong premise? What if I haven't been given the right family story?*

~

As the plane descends back into Melbourne, I carry not only the lovely pleasure of reuniting with extended family—*damn, I didn't ask Helen about the origins of our connection!*—but also the weight of the most pressing question, the one that led me to Hobart. The more I seek, the less I feel I know about what to do.

This morning, I had probed Helen further about whether Mum had confided in her at the time about Grant. She'd reiterated that Mum and Dad had taken the doctors' advice on Grant's Down Syndrome condition very seriously. It was acute and his life expectancy would be brief.

'But why did they keep the secret from me? Why didn't they tell me when I first asked? Why didn't Mum take me with you both when you went to visit Grant?'

My plea to Helen sounds like I want her to take me now.

'Your parents truly believed he wouldn't live long, so there was no point in telling you as a child.'

'But he did live. He was still alive when I was seventeen and discovered my birth certificate and still, they maintained the silence. Why? I don't understand.'

'Your mother wanted you to have a life free of responsibility for

Grant. If he had outlived them, she didn't want you to be left with the burden for his care. It was how things were done back then.'

'I have one final question, Helen. Do you think I should go and meet Grant now?'

After a long pause of inaudible thinking music, Helen raised her head. Her wise gaze met my childlike eyes, and her very firm reply was, 'No, I don't believe you should go. What's in the past must stay in the past. It's what your mother wanted.'

And with that, the conversation ended.

~

Continuing my reading years later, in 2021, I learn that the first goal of Family Constellations is to make the invisible visible, which is something I remembered both Judith Glaser and Dr David speaking about. I'm discovering there were many parts of my story kept out of sight. The second goal is to find a way to resolve the fear that began in the past. Sélénée's book offers me a way to give every family member the belonging and rightful place they were denied. In doing so, I can restore order.

This is all fine, but none of my displaced family members are still alive. How is it possible to find the resolution these authors speak of? *Keep reading, continue to learn, ask Sarah,* I imagine Chris urging. The resolution that Marine Sélénée refers to releases any unconscious loyalties that we may have been carrying. Sarah helps me to see it hasn't been my guilt I've been living with for as long as I can remember, but possibly my mother's. *And was she carrying ancestral guilt?*

I would never have described the broader term 'family' as a system. Thinking about it now, a system comprises a group of individual parts forming a unified whole, and consequently is greater than the sum of its parts. Those singular parts are dependent on each other to function, and the system is powered by the dynamic of that interdependence. Systems are about the collective versus the individual. I can see this very clearly with John's family in Perth. When one of them falls, the others come together with the strength of spiders to repair any damage to the web.

I still have doubts about this new thinking. It's predicated on the impact of trauma, but I have no memory of experiencing a 'trauma'. Sarah explains that traumatic events are difficult to define because the same event may be more traumatic for one person than another. Mark Wolynn says a well-documented feature of trauma is our inability to articulate what happens to us. And not only do we lose our words, but our memory as well. This sounds like when I've been triggered at the dentist and I lose my capacity to speak, yet in that moment I have no memory connected to why it's happening.

Marine agrees with Mark, and their words resonate with me so intimately that they have come to feel like friends. They both refer to the new research in epigenetics that supports the systemic view that an individual's struggles are a by-product of a deeper shared family legacy by demonstrating the inheritability of trauma at the cellular level.

I've inherited brown eyes from my father's family. Has my body also inherited what Elly and Ludwig suffered in Nazi Germany, what Dad endured in the internment camp? Or am I grasping at ideas to assuage my own guilt of remaining loyal to the decisions of my parents by not going to meet Grant?

What's starting to emerge from the formal programs I've completed, and this new reading, is a clarity about how I've been functioning in the world. A picture is forming of the collective wounds of my ancestors that were never healed. Mark and Marine both found in their experience, and state clearly, that an only child often carries these burdens from the past into the present.

CHAPTER 25

Survivors

It's October 2022, and as I walk into the Mornington library, I'm intentionally checking in emotionally and steadying myself. This is a first. I don't go to libraries as a rule, so I miss events and exhibitions that potentially could be important. The library aversion goes back decades, and I'm guessing it's related to my teaching years, including the office I had with a window exposing me to every student who walked through its doors. It holds the place in my memory as being the site from where I made the phone call to the Genetic Clinic and then my mother; the calls that halted my journey to motherhood.

The Scheibner family narrative has been growing and gaining colour and shape since I met Dr Anna Hirsch and took on the challenge of writing Dad's timeline. It seems appropriate, in fact, essential that today I bring myself to the travelling exhibition, *Let Me Be Myself – The Life Story of Anne Frank*. Libraries have a particular feeling born of the nature of those who work in them. Serious yet accessible, quiet but not silent, respectful and inviting. There are still rows and shelves of hard book copies promising learning as well as entertainment. The large windows allow natural light to shine between and on the rows of the display. I begin my journey into history.

~

It's mid-2021 and we're locked down again. I'm reading more and noticing an invisible aerial working overtime, drawing my attention to things I would have previously been blind to. One of those is an email from my local independent bookshop, Farrell's, promoting new releases. An unseen magnet draws me to 'The Survivors' by Adam P Frankel, a story of war, inheritance and healing. The back of book blurb calls out, *A Memoir of Family, The Holocaust, Trauma and Identity*. It's outside business hours but the urgency to learn more takes me to a Google search where I find a YouTube interview the author did with former PepsiCo CEO, Indra Nooyi.

Despite being born two generations after me, and coming from a completely different career working as deputy speechwriter for Barack Obama during his first term as President, I feel instantly drawn to Adam Frankel. Not because the unfolding story is the same as mine, but because I can feel the implications of the words and phrases he's using. His mother kept a secret from him, his father and the whole family. After she finally revealed the secret, he says he essentially experienced an identity crisis. It took him years to get the detail from her, and another decade before he found the inner nerve to get a paternity test which proved the father he loved dearly was not his biological father.

As he went through the process of trying to understand how this happened and why his mother had never revealed the truth, he went back to his maternal grandparents Bubbe and Zayde who were Holocaust survivors of various Nazi concentration camps and labour camps. Unlike Elly and Ludwig, my grandparents, Bubbe and Zayde survived to immigrate to America where his mother was born. His mother was the daughter of Holocaust survivors and Adam recounts snippets of the horror his grandparents lived through and adds that these trauma stories were part the Jewish community. It was the legacy he grew up with.

She asks him if he thinks the trauma of the Holocaust is passed down. Was it part of his family story and how did he make the connection? I'm enthralled with this conversation and feel a sense of validation when Adam says we now know more about trauma and intergenerational trauma than we've ever known. When he decided to write his story, wanting to learn more about intergenerational trauma led him to Dr Rachel Yehuda, the same researcher I'd been introduced to by Judith Glasser and Mark Wolynn. Dr Yehuda told Adam that trauma is basically described and understood as a watershed event that defines your life and divides it into a before and after. Might that explain why Dad's story, as told to me, began when he met Mum, not long after his release from internment?

I listen carefully as Adam tells the audience how Dr Yehuda has done cutting edge research in the emerging field of epigenetics. She found the epigenome, a layer of information that sits on top of the gene and can be affected by external factors like diet, pollution, chronic stress and trauma. She found that children of Holocaust survivors are three times more likely to display symptoms of PTSD when exposed to traumatic events than similar aged people who are not children of Holocaust survivors. Dr Yehuda found that children of women who were pregnant on September 11 and near Ground Zero have displayed similarly low levels of cortisol as their parents, consistent with PTSD. So, we know trauma can leave a genetic impact and can be passed down. How it's passed down is still open to scrutiny and debate. We also know, through other research, that the way families respond to trauma can have impacts on the likelihood of their children developing mental health issues, including anxiety, like Adam's mother did. I wonder if the lethargy, fainting and exhaustion of my teenage school years that became more serious at university, often keeping me bedbound for several days, was depression. I wonder if the panic attack I had on a flight from Italy back to England, when the flight attendant had to take me to the front of the plane to care for me because I couldn't breathe, was anxiety?

If I wasn't sure before, I certainly am now. I want to read Adam Frankel's memoir. Apart from brief case studies and quoted research, this is the first person I've witnessed telling their story of the impact coming down through generations from the Holocaust. I'm not alone, I can relate to another individual's family story. I'm jotting down questions and noting parallels. Although he was raised alongside his grandparents, Bubbe and Zayde, and their recollections, he knew there were secrets. His mother recalls that for much of her childhood, they rarely talked about their own experiences, and the children learnt not to push.

And in the same way I hadn't connected the dots, he says looking back there were dots he didn't connect. He says as a kid, he knew there was stuff you didn't talk about. Somebody would ask a question and conversation would be shut off. He absorbed it and says he was not fully dialled into what was going on. Yes! I believe that describes me perfectly.

When Adam's mother finally revealed the truth of his paternity, he was so angry he stopped speaking to her. I didn't stop speaking to my parents when they told me Grant had not died as a baby, but I shut off and buried their shame. I was still living under their roof, and not yet the adult Adam had been, but something shifted in me and the lesson of not questioning was cemented. Yet I felt different about myself and about them.

~

The exhibition features a reproduction of Anne Frank's original diary and photographs of her abridged life, as well as World War II memorabilia. The starting point is marked with a huge black and white photo of Anne at a school desk looking directly into the camera. Her smile, with just enough teeth showing to look content, belies the despondency of the times. Holding a pencil, she's looked up from writing for the photographer. I wonder what she's thinking.

Moving on, I pause at each panel containing images and texts about the world around Anne: the rise of Hitler, the persecution of the Jews and the war. The aim of the Anne Frank Stichting (Foundation) responsible for the exhibition is to illustrate how the lives of persecuted people such as the Frank family were affected by the political events of the 1930s and 1940s. I'm filtering all this for the first time through the eyes of my dad, Elly and Ludwig, despite hearing Anne's story before. When I was living in England, one of the many trips I did was to Amsterdam where I visited the Anne Frank House Museum. Today is different, there's a disturbance under my skin. I'm experiencing a display that 'invites visitors to contemplate diversity, identity, prejudice, equal rights, and democracy', and my reflections on how unsafe it was to be different, to be Jewish, now have a new meaning.

Choosing the beach route for the walk home, in preference to the hustle of Main Street, I hope I can defrag and reground from the war years back into 2022. I still feel regretful that I wasn't given an opportunity to learn and understand this part of my heritage. I think back to Robyn Beckmann and other Jewish school friends and wonder what their family stories entailed. My musings are tarnished by the shame of it not occurring to me to even ask. I think about Dad's efforts to disguise his origins, and I'm beginning to see his courage and bravery rather than his deliberate withholding. I can see how, as an only child, he, too, would have been lonely and later isolated.

~

The trauma of war and the Holocaust was more pervasive in Adam Frankel's childhood than mine. But another central takeaway from this interview is familiar. Adam describes interviewing his mother's closest friends for the book. They had known her at the time he was a baby and described her as being terrified and haunted that people would find out. During my conversations with Sarah, we talked about my dad learning not to talk about his heritage in case the authorities found out. By the time Grant was born, Dad knew no other way but to keep the truth silent.

There have been many ideas, awakenings and musings since COVID and especially since Chris passed away. On the one hand, learning theories and reading research from Judith Glaser, David Drake and Mark Wolynn have expanded my professional tool kit. On the other hand, Sarah has been my interpreter, helping me understand the crossovers from professional to personal. When Adam Frankel says it was tough to see trauma passed down generations, he also began to recognise the way it reverberates, strains relationships and creates all kinds of aftereffects that can't be foreseen. The revelation about his birth shook his sense of self and identity. I sense I'm creeping closer to resolving the empty spaces I first defined amid the darkness of the grief of losing Chris. I search LinkedIn for Adam P Frankel and send him a request to connect, but oddly, I already feel connected to him.

CHAPTER 26

Family Secrets

Journal entry, March 2022.

I've just discovered a podcast series. The voice in my AirPods is gentle and composed. She's quietly telling me that this is Family Secrets, secrets that are kept from us, secrets we keep from others and the secrets we keep from ourselves. While the discovery of family secrets can initially be terrifying or traumatic, often these discoveries have the power to liberate, heal and even uplift us.

Thank you, Dani Shapiro! You've opened a vault and I want to get inside and explore.

We all have family secrets. This is not a new concept to me. So why am I astonished at the number of listeners this podcast is pulling? There have been over 22 million downloads across six seasons of Family Secrets since it launched in 2021. I'm not alone then.

First though, I'm curious about Dani Shapiro. I can see she's won a National Jewish Book Award for fiction. More digging and yes, I see she, too, has written a memoir with the resonating title, *'Inheritance: A Memoir of Genealogy, Paternity and Love'*. The graphic depicted on the cover suggests a family tree. Inside the fly cover, I'm drawn to the words *'submitted her DNA to a family genealogy website for analysis'*. Here we go. I'm ready for this. Am I drawing these authors to me for a reason, or is this all a coincidence and I'm reading too much into it?

My work with Sarah has uncovered a compassion for my parents that has been absent in the past. Rather than blocking any thoughts about them, I'm finding a fresh curiosity for the decisions they made.

I've learnt that not revealing the truth of Grant's condition at birth and their choice to give him up was to protect me. More significantly, secrets of this enormity weigh heavily on the keeper and are often carried alone or in my mum and dad's case, kept within the sanctity of their marriage. Did it bind them together more? Can secrets create internal conflicts, leading to stress, anxiety, and a sense of isolation? Were secrets the cause of the uneasy tension between my father and my aunt?

As I scroll down the menu of past recordings looking for an episode that might have a private meaning for me, like the story of a missing sibling, I'm drawn to the title *"Bubbe and Zayde and Grandma and Pa" a conversation with Adam Frankel*. Fabulous! I've not long finished reading his memoir, *'The Survivors'*, and am keen to hear him discuss it now that I know the complete story. I was always the person who didn't ever write in or highlight books in any way. Books were for reading not writing in, but in the last couple of years that belief has been smashed. Books are now my lifeline, helping me reconstruct the meaning of my life. I'm not alone. I most likely will never meet Adam Frankel, but I feel an honest affinity with him. My copy of *'The Survivors'* is underlined from page one, line one of the Preface: *'This is not the book I intended to write.'* In the margin, I've pencilled, *And my life is not the life I intended to live.*

Listening to these two authors sharing a microphone, probably in a studio somewhere in New York City, in a different time zone, calmly discussing secrets, is mesmerising. I can't get enough of this stuff. It reminds me of when I first met Sarah and the energy I always felt leaving her office having been heard, having been taught that I haven't failed at doing adult life. It's an energy that has still not left me even though we now meet online. Quickly opening a new page in my journal, I want to get down all the gems I'm hearing from my two new 'friends', Dani and Adam.

Adam Frankel writes and talks about secrets being part of his family's tradition and, indeed, part of every family. But he says there's something very pronounced about the way *'Holocaust families tend to their secrets'*. The phrase is poignant, and his words paint fields of red poppies for me, like the first flowers to spring up after World War I in the barren battlefields of northern France and Belgium. It reminds me of the elderly Jewish men and women balancing on stools at the too tall table in the archive department of the Holocaust Museum in Melbourne. They were digging, pruning and nurturing history as they translated the fields of documents for tomorrow's visitors in order to keep the truth alive.

I've missed the question, but Adam is saying he hasn't known the truth of himself most of his life. After his mother told him, he absorbed the secret of his real father and moved on. That's what they did in his family and that's what I learnt in mine. Don't ask questions, don't tell anybody. This was his frame of reference for processing secrets and it's exactly what I did after I learnt about Grant. Just like Adam, I didn't know what to do with the information of Grant's reveal when I was eighteen, so I stopped asking questions, buried it and moved on. It was nearly two decades before I asked Mum again. I absorbed her response and for the second time moved on. Was that a sliding door moment in my life? My mind has been wandering in all directions during this podcast. I refocus in time to hear Adam telling Dani about when he finally realised that he was now keeping the secret that had been kept from him. Sarah helped me see this is what loyal obedient kids do. And when Adam says he never got the whole story from anybody, I write down Helen, Auntie Orm, oldest cousin Max. At least three people could have helped me get the whole story. I wonder if there were others. The solicitor who handled Mum's will? She must have known the truth about both Daphne and Grant because she also helped Mum challenge Great Grandmother Flora's will.

Gosh, what was the last part of that sentence? I rewind to when Adam realised the secret was a blockage and the spillover effect had been huge in his life. He'd ended his relationship at the time and was struggling with the truth on his own. Finding the courage to tell the dad who'd raised him that he wasn't his biological dad became a pivotal moment for Adam. It was the part that had been missing. He adds that writing his story was essential to processing and moving on. He says, 'It was a jumble of information I didn't know how to disentangle.'

Hearing the word 'disentangle', I hit the pause button and belt to my office to find my A3 sketchpad. I'd started using it to mind map

ideas for speaking topics when I was preparing for the Bali trip just
before COVID closed borders and put a halt to air travel. Thankful
for my habit of adding the date to a new entry, I see the themes in
2019 related to my work as a personal branding strategist. In 2021, I
added the *Iceberg* to chronicle all the jigsaw pieces coming to life as
I worked my way through the list of family questions in Part One of
Mark Wolynn's book, *'It Didn't Start with You'*. Turning to a fresh page
headed *Disentangling*, I draw a Venn diagram and write 'ME' in the
centre. I name the left circle *Life Events*, the right circle *Themes* and
the bottom circle holding the top two up becomes *Secrets*. Across the
bottom of this page, I repeat the phrase Judith Glasser repeatedly used:
Moving from the Invisible to the Visible. Allowing myself a five-minute
break from the podcast, and grabbing my pens of many colours, I
move quickly, arranging words, concepts and ideas around the page.
The story of my life that I'd believed was normal and uninteresting,
rendering me invisible, was taking on an unexpected character.

Back to the pod. Adam is talking about the overwhelm of
disentangling everything he learnt after the secret was out. It was detail
about his identity that he hadn't known how to fit together and had him
repeatedly asking, who am I? Funny thing is I'd read this in his book,
but today I'm hearing it differently. He uses the word 'threads' and I've
just used the word 'themes'. I like his word better. Metaphorically, I can
see the invisible threads tying me to the past in ways I couldn't possibly
have noticed growing up.

~

I've always been a reader who enjoyed autobiographies and
biographies as well as fiction. I've always been a fan of movies and TV
drama, too. But I've never read or watched a story I could relate to as
personally and directly as the memoirs I'm discovering now. In the
past, the storylines would always trigger the pain of loss and regret for
what I hadn't experienced in my life rather than what I had. Neither
'Inheritance' or *'The Survivors'* are my story, but I feel every breath of
expanding clarity as the authors search to comprehend the meaning of
their circumstances.

I've listened to her podcasts and read her book and Instagram posts, so can't be sure where I heard her talk about secrets like this, but somewhere, Dani Shapiro says: *Anything we can't understand become secrets.* This is thought provoking. Is that what I've been doing? Rather than blaming my parents for their silence, have I been withholding part of myself from others because I haven't understood my own choices and behaviours?

Dani Shapiro talks about becoming a student of secrets. Both she and Adam Frankel find themselves striving to unravel their identities in the wake of their family secrets. As Dani acknowledges, throughout history, great minds have grappled with the notion of identity. A stranger sending DNA test results from a laboratory can tell a more complete story of you, and genetically speaking I was half Ashkenazi Jewish. The unseen genetic code of previous generations can subvert our emotional identity through epigenetic changes. I'm sure I recall learning about samskaras in Indian philosophy at university, the concept of mental, emotional and behavioural traits inherited across generations. The notion that the grief I lived with didn't belong to me is becoming more visible now.

In my first conversations with Sarah, we talked about the many gaps I'd felt which I described to her as empty spaces in my heart. The loss of Chris, Grant, the babies I'd never had, I'd translated all this as evidence that I'd never been enough for someone to love with all their heart, to want to marry, to start and grow a family with me. That was how I identified myself. It's what I believed. To protect the secret of my unworthiness, I adopted a professional persona that was polished enough to throw people off the scent of my personal inadequacies. Yet now, as I reassemble and re understand my life, I'm extricating a more multi-layered identity. The revelations of the last few years have been moving me away from the silence of my family secrets, allowing me to recognise that I can break the threads that have linked me back to the past. I feel like I'm being propelled forward to what I can only describe as a profound sense of self-identity.

Returning to my sketchbook, I draw a line dividing the new page into two halves. The left column is *Name, Rank and Serial number*. The right column becomes *Self-Identity/ WHO do I think I am?*

Part Three

Belonging

"There are far better things ahead than those we leave behind."
C. S. Lewis

CHAPTER 27

Identification

Midsummer 2016, and Chris has passed away. In all cultures, families gather to mourn, honour and nourish those who grieve. Depending on the choice of faith, preparations are made for the family to farewell the deceased. Chris made amends with God in the final weeks and chose an Anglican funeral despite being raised a Catholic. With catdog Kev on my lap now, wondering where his other human is, I make the notification calls to those awaiting the news and those who thought he'd live forever.

The logical, organised person at my side is Bec. Her capability and her familiarity with the practicalities of church management allow space for me to breathe. Before Mum died, she asked my cousin John to look after me in life and so he's here from Perth, too, an angel quietly making cups of tea materialise and ensuring I'm sustained. Each day, the constant requirement to make another important decision is wearing me down. Chris has deserted me. I'm a solitary entity detached from the love of those around me, doing this alone.

~

Dear Chris,

That was then, and I wish I could tell you how I feel now. You'd be very impressed with the contents of my heaving bookshelf. All the leadership and personal branding titles have been moved to lower levels, and now, within line of sight, are books that are expanding my mind, digging new neural pathways and shifting my heart. Sitting alongside our favourite 'Reinventing Your Life' is 'The Body Keeps Score: Brain, Mind, and Body in the Healing of Trauma' by Bessel van der Kolk, which was a recommendation from your long-time fly-fishing mate, Alan Morrison.

Look at these recent additions:

'When the Body Says No: The Cost of Hidden Stress' by Gabor Mate

'What Happened to You? Conversations on Trauma, Resilience and Healing' by Dr Bruce D Perry and Oprah Winfrey

'You're Not Broken: Break free from trauma and reclaim your life' by Dr Sarah Woodhouse

'Connected Fates, Separate Destinies: Using Family Constellations Therapy to Recover from Inherited Stories and Trauma' by Marine Sélénée

'It Didn't Start with You: How inherited family trauma shapes who we are and how to end the cycle' by Mark Wolynn

Chris, you'd be fascinated with Mark's book. Although first published in 2016, I didn't discover it until 2021. How many hours do you think we spent sharing our grumbles about families? And how odd did we think it was that Paul's memories of your childhood were so different to yours? How often did you tell me your Crohn's disease flareups were triggered by stress? And remember how you journeyed with me through the awakenings about Grant? This book offers us a new lens of understanding and shifts all those conversations away from regret toward solutions and the possibility of healing.

You loved quotes and Mark leads us into the view he's encountered through his own experience, years of work with clients and research, with this:

'The most powerful ties are the ones to the people who gave us birth … it hardly seems to matter how many years have passed, how many betrayals there may have been, how much misery in the family: We remain connected, even against our wills.'

Anthony Brandt, 'Bloodlines'

How is this relevant to you or me? I'm learning that we can biologically inherit the obsessive thoughts that we think are ours, the fears and anxieties, from our parents and our grandparents' symptoms. So, along with physical attributes like eye colour, there are four unconscious themes that can disrupt the positive life flow coming down the family pipeline. This is especially likely when any trauma was not talked about, like the secret of Grant or when healing has been incomplete. When healing cannot occur, there's every chance one or more of these four themes are at work.

1. Merged with a parent.
2. Rejected a parent.
3. Experienced a break in the early bond with our mother.
4. Identified with a member of our family system other than our parents.

When you and I talked about family, we meant parents and our own line on the family tree. Theorists like Mark Wolynn say it's much broader, that everyone impacts and influences our familial relationships, including grandparents, siblings, aunts, uncles, aborted/miscarried/stillborn children, former partners, ancestors who lived challenging lives, faced disabilities, or experienced war-related events, plus any family secrets and excluded family members.

The book is a guide with case studies, exercises and questions to help us understand whether any of the unconscious themes are a fit. I eliminate the first two and feel myself rejecting the third theme of a break in the bond between me and Mum. I can't believe Esmee didn't mother well (she died before I met you, so you probably didn't realise I called her by her Christian name in preference to Mum). When I studied Narrative Coaching, Dr David Drake devoted a module to Attachment Theory because it supplements our understanding of the undercurrents in the preverbal roots of our stories and actions. I had a blind spot to this content at the time and wouldn't read it. One thing that did stand out, though, is that significant experiences when we are young have a disproportionate impact on our development and identity. It does make me think about Auntie Daphne and my aversion to her. What's that persistent twinge now, though?

After you passed away, I was left with a chasm that couldn't be filled. You know I've searched out counsellors over the years, as we both did, and this time, I found my wonderful Sarah. There's been many lightbulb moments in our sessions, including when she asked me to imagine what it must have been like for Mum during her pregnancy with me, hoping for nine months that this time she'd have a normal healthy baby. So, when Mark Wolynn asks, 'Did something traumatic happen while your mother was pregnant with you? Was she highly anxious, depressed, or stressed?', I read it as a version of Sarah's prompt.

I've long tossed around the possibility of a link in my mind between Grant's genetic condition and Daphne's mystery illness somehow leading me to subconsciously deciding not to have children. What if his absence from my childhood limited me as an adult in other ways in order to hold my childlessness safe?

The book asks,

- Could you be feeling like, behaving like, suffering like, atoning for, or carrying the grief for someone who came before you?
  As a child I had an affinity to Grandmother Elly despite never meeting her?
- Do you have symptoms, feelings, or behaviours that are difficult to explain in the context of your life experience?
  Most definitely! Constant melancholy, loss and aloneness.
- Did guilt or pain prevent a family member from loving someone or grieving his or her loss?
  The secret of Grant must have stifled my parents' capacity to grieve.
- Was there a trauma in the family (an early death of a parent, child, or sibling, or an abandonment), an event that was too terrible, painful, or shameful to talk about?
  Does my feeling of abandonment belong to Grant?
- Could you be connected with that event, living a life similar to the person no one talks about?
  How many times did we talk about how I didn't feel connected to my family? Remember how you wanted to tell John after many of those incidents and I stopped you?

The more I submerge into the book, having worked with these questions, the more I'm convinced that it's highly likely I've identified with Grant. When he was sent to Kew Cottages, it was a rejection from our family. I grew up knowing there was a gap and a topic never to speak of. And I'm convinced my parents didn't heal the pain or the shame of their decision and I didn't move forward into the life they would have wished for me. Identification with the missing or rejected baby is likely when a first child 'dies' or is sent from the family system and parents fall pregnant straight away. How often have you heard me quip that I was the replacement baby? And when a woman doesn't have male siblings, there's a likelihood of identification or merging with a male in the family system!

Boom! That's got to be it.

Chris, I wish we could work this through together like we did in 2010 with 'Reinvent Your Life'. It was the first time I'd recognised any underlying drivers of the constant insecurities that plagued all my relationships. Jeffrey Young called it the Abandonment Lifetrap and the phrase entered our lexicon. Mark Wolynn is fleshing it out, but I can't imagine how I'm going to explain this to the Perth family without telling them how it's been for me for years.

Writing this letter that I can never post keeps you on my shoulder, overseeing my transition away from life ache and toward life ease. We shared a crusade to keep pushing forward to understand and heal disharmonious connections with others. I think this new perspective would have been a source of healing and resolution for you, too.

Can I offer you one of your own quotes?

'Life must be understood backwards, but it must be lived forward.'

Soren Kierkegaard (Danish theologian and philosopher)

Forever,

Mish x

~

The day is hugging warm, just the right temperature for a walk with an audiobook. Re-reading my letter to Chris reminds me of the self-version I wore in the world every day, right up to meeting Sarah. With clients, I was positive and encouraging as I urged them to trust themselves and create possibility. With myself, I welcomed the nagging inner chat of a long list of complaints. My journalling always brought me back to the same place. Why couldn't others understand what my life was like? The mantra was, *I wish they could walk in my footsteps for just one day.* This was amplified the first time I went to Perth after I lost Chris, and I was trying to explain that I wasn't all right. No one heard. Purely and simply, I didn't have the language, let alone the concepts to help others grasp the world I lived in.

I want to shake this version of me off, the version that didn't start with me. It's a workday, inside school hours, outside dog walking times. I'm alone with my beliefs and Mark Wolynn's voice in my ear with his even tempo as he says, so how do we know if you and I have inherited family trauma? Most of us carry trauma language, our core complaints, descriptors and traumas are hidden inside the words and phrases we use, rinse and repeat.

Finding a beach box with a timber deck jutting out into the sand, I prop on the step. Grateful to have brought my journal so I can complete the exercise, the voice in my ear is now explaining. At the top of the page, I write, *Investigating Your Core Complaint.*

To begin, focus on a problem that's most pressing in your life right now. It might be an issue with your health, your job, your relationship—any issue that disrupts your sense of safety, peace, security, or well-being.

The problem is I'm single, have never married, have never felt secure in any relationship, have never felt what it's like to be one hundred per cent special, significant in love.

Don't edit yourself, write it down as it comes to you.

What is the deepest issue you want to heal? Maybe it's a problem that feels overwhelming to you. Maybe it's a symptom or a feeling you've had all your life.

All my life, feeling sad, lonely and alone have been with me, like familiar friends who can appear in an instant. I want to shift this feeling of reliance on self. Everyone else puts someone before me. Always has. It's usually their children and it's felt like I wasn't good enough, strong enough, generous enough, loving enough to be a mother. I don't know how to be a totally loving mother or a totally loving daughter or a loving partner. It's like my efforts were always overcome by my own limited belief in self. I want to heal the unworthiness of this.

Relationships, both personal and professional, fracture because I always overreact when I sense someone is withholding information, or I find out later and shut down and get lost in my head. How many times have I lamented, 'Why wasn't I told?'

If the feeling or symptom you have never goes away, what would you be afraid could happen to you?

I might choke and die at home, and it could be days and weeks before anyone would know. There will be no one to lovingly help me and partner me on a daily or nightly basis out of my pain, fear and anxiety. There would be no loving partner or child to will me safely and painlessly to heaven like I did for Chris.

What would be the worst thing about dying alone?

If this state continues, I will die alone, will be forgotten, will have left no legacy and it will be the end of the Scheibner story. It won't be long before no one remembers me.

The final word I hear from Mark Wolynn before hitting stop on what's been a heart wrenching thirty minutes is, life sends us forward with something unresolved from the past. I know the healing has begun and I'm moving forward into a resolved life.

CHAPTER 28

Swiss Cheese

It's 6:55 am on April 2021, and I've been up for a couple of hours, the anticipation ejecting me from bed long before any alarm is needed. This is a special day. By the time I'd finished working through Mark Wolynn's book *'It Didn't Start with You'*, I'd formed a different perspective about the complaints, regrets and fears that had been keeping me awake every night since Chris passed away. Despite Sarah's expertise interpreting my life story through this framework, I still wonder if I'm a fraud. There's a nagging doubt that maybe I've grasped this theory too readily. After all, I hadn't lived through any trauma, Dad had escaped the Holocaust and Grant was of my generation.

Three weeks ago, I resolved to try and have a session with Mark Wolynn himself, so we could go through my story together. He could hear my conclusions and either validate or dismiss my interpretation. I'd now completed all the exercises, starting with the core complaint. From there, I kept journalling until I uncovered my core sentence, and my fear was revealed. It led me straight back to Grant.

Searching Mark's website for an email address, I'd sent a request. The reply was short. He was unavailable and his assistant Kari Dunlop was running these sessions now. She had worked with Mark for ten years after completing her own journey and had found a place of healing with him as her guide. So, I booked and today is the day. I'm about to meet Kari to test and unravel my story.

In order to come to the session prepared, Kari has asked me to complete all the questions in Mark's book, which I have reviewed. In all the research I've been immersed in, the most powerful revelations can be summed up in three points, pushing me to new thinking about the impact of trauma on my life:

1. How our mother bonds with us in the womb is instrumental in the development of our neural chemistry. The bond with our mother is the template for how we show up in our future life. This is the one key point I have not accepted. My relationship with Mum was pretty normal, despite as an adult, observing others mothering in a very different way. I explained it to myself as being a generational thing—which I'm sure is partly true.

2. Issues arise when the event or story within the family system remains unknown, unacknowledged and unresolved. I've been uncovering and grappling with the secrets I knew, as well as those I didn't. Some remain unknown, like the two boys, Reuben and William, along with Martha, their sister, named in Great Grandmother Flora's death notice as siblings of Kitty and Daphne. They must have died as babies.

3. Trauma is instinctively about repetition. Look for negative repetitions and patterns in your life. My detective work has identified a pattern of isolation and disconnection on the family tree with Elly, Judaism and Grant.

~

As I click the link and Zoom goes through its screens, I pray for clarity and confirmation. Then Kari Dunlop appears. Her manner is relaxed and friendly, her tone calm and measured. I'm so hyped up and eager that I can hear myself speaking unnecessarily loudly but can't pause to modulate. Kari listens intently so she can create a family picture of all the critical players, but I'm still too wedded to the details of my story to hear what's inside the facts. I've forgotten Dr David Drake's teaching, that in this moment it's not the story itself, it's how the experience of the story makes us feel. I'd been feeling overwhelmed yet detached from those players.

Then Kari asks, 'If your life suddenly fell apart, what's your worst fear? What's the worst thing that could happen to you? The answer to this question is key.'

'I'd be abandoned, I'll die alone, and it will be *like I'll be forgotten*,' and as I hear the words fall out, I feel the burn of tears forcing their way out, too. I gasp and my right hand jumps to my throat, and the left covers my heart. I recognise this as a mannerism I've repeated thousands of times. Don't know when it began, but it's my anchor whenever anxiety escalates.

'What are you feeling right now, as you hear those words?' she asks, recognising my body response, an indication that we've hit something important.

'It's the first time I've actually heard myself say this. When I was doing the homework, I was thinking about not leaving a legacy. Saying *like I never existed* feels way deeper!'

Until talking to Kari, I'd connected the fear of dying alone to Grant being alone in hospital without family at his bedside. I'd remembered Mum waiting until I'd left after midnight and dying in hospital alone, too.

Kari explains being alone probably comes from even earlier, before Grant. We were looking for who was abandoned not remembered. Now I was thinking about Elly and Ludwig. Men and women were separated in death camps, so Elly would have died alone, not wrapped in Ludwig's arms for protection.

After another set of forensic questions to connect those dots, Kari has pinpointed that I don't know who Reuben, William and Martha's father was. Another male missing in terms of the story, so unable to be considered and unable to leave a legacy in the family. She then asked about mum, how we got on and if she was a good mum? Also, about how she got on with her mum?

'She was a good mum, yes. My memory of growing up is there wasn't much emoting or loving, no pictures of me sitting on her knee while she read me a story or soothed my tears. I was happy to leave home before entering my twenties and could not have gone back, but my adult relationship with her was good. I am my mother in the sense that she was a compromiser.'

I know Kari doesn't need more details, so I stop oversharing.

'Okay, because they gave your brother away, it would make it very hard for your mother to give to you. There wouldn't be a lot of juice left for mothering because her unconscious guilt or shame was at play. Plus, you would remind her of the fear and trauma of the decision.'

Kari explains that as early as twenty days' gestation, the cells that become our nervous system are developed. So, of course, there's no cognitive memory, but it's being laid down as a somatic soundtrack and shows up in us later in life. She tells me about a study establishing how babies go into fight or flight because of the stress, fear and acute worry of whatever their mother is encountering. Baby is just marinating in cortisol and adrenaline in the womb and, even this early, begins to organise itself around mum's feelings.

She reminds me of something I read in 'When the Body Says No'. Gabor Mate believes our first nine months of life are like a second gestation for the baby. It's when much of our neural development is happening. Baby's prefrontal cortex gets tuned by mum's feeling states, so if mother is unable to be present, our self-worth can't develop.

'Earlier you described yourself as very independent,' observes Kari, and I nod agreement. 'Bert Hellinger describes the reaching out of a baby's natural movement as being like they're expanding into life. It's like here I am, I've arrived. But when a mum is lost in her grief and her sadness, baby shrinks and defences start to form: I won't ask for help, I'm independent, I won't trust that she can take care of me.'

It really hits a nerve when Kari asks me to watch a video. It's Dr Edward Tronick's 'still face' experiment. Dr Tronick conducted experiments to show how babies are extremely responsive to the emotions and interactions around them. I watch a mother crouching down in front of the stroller, facing her twelve-month-old child. The mother has the widest smile as she plays with her little girl. Baby stretches toward her giggling, then points out into the room. The mother turns to look, too, and engages with the game. It's a beautiful exchange seeing mother and baby working together to coordinate their emotions and forming and strengthening the bond between them.

Then mum is asked to stop responding and to hold a neutral face as if she can't see her daughter's need. The child quickly picks up on this and uses all her abilities, smiling and pointing, to try to get mother back. With mum maintaining her stillness, the baby makes screechy sounds, squealing at the mother, like 'come on why aren't we doing this?' Then Dr Tronick explains that, even in these two minutes, when they don't get the normal reaction, babies react with negative emotions. They turn away and they actually may lose control of their posture because of the stress they're experiencing. Then mother resumes their play, and all is back to how it was. I can't hold back tears now. I feel every cry of the baby struggling to hold her mother's eye contact and attention. Not because a maternal instinct kicks in, but because deep down in my soul, it feels so familiar.

Mark Wolynn and Kari describe this bond as critical to the development of the baby's core. If our physical core is the central part of our body, crucial to effectively holding us up, then our inner core is our central sense of self, our inner nurturer that holds us up emotionally from within. A break in attachment creates holes in this core like Swiss cheese and leads to a break with ourselves. Baby can't feel mum, so feels into the messages of something is wrong with me. That's where the feelings of not being enough, I don't matter, come from. Baby seeks validation and works to please mum and make her happy. Growing up from this foundation we become experienced at reading the field in front of us, not knowing what version of mum we are going to get. So we become exceptionally sensitive to the emotions of those around us and often work in roles requiring empathy.

Kari clarifies, 'So, a break in the bond can happen developmentally anytime from zero to age ten. But we can inherit it, too. We can hear this possibly with your mum and her mother, and the likelihood of your dad with his mum, Elly. She turned her back on her faith, family and most likely was consumed with hiding the truth of her Jewish family whilst protecting and ensuring she and her baby survived in a new country. We do hear developmental trauma with you and also a likely unconscious loyalty not wanting to recognise that your mother couldn't keep her child or couldn't mother.'

Now I'm wondering again what happened to Martha, William and Reuben? How do I find out? As Dani Shapiro says, once a secret is exposed, more comes to light over time.

My first answer when asked what was the core complaint I wanted to resolve was relationships. Mother is also the blueprint for our intimate relationships. We know if she is cold to us, we project this on to our partners. I know outsiders wouldn't have been privy to the times when Mum was 'cold' and silent with me. She was never a hugger. She always kept her emotions in check. Even at Dad's funeral she pulled away from me. I can see this in my own reactions to those close to me.

'If we can't receive from mother, we can't receive from life, and that includes relationships,' Kari adds. 'We become people pleasers and avoid conflict, have no boundaries in relationships, get into bad relationships because someone is "seeing" us and "lighting" us up. We didn't get the "lighting up" that happens between mothers and babies.'

This is how I landed in that unequal affair in my first year of teaching and again with Matthew. In both these situations, very handsome men were 'seeing' me in a way no one had ever before and initially it 'lit' me up—it was like a drug to me, until it wasn't. I couldn't advocate for myself and my behaviours stemmed from insecurity. Better to be seen than not seen, even if it eventually faded and ended in buckets of tears.

Kari moves on to my parents' relationship.

I give her the facts of their meeting as my best guess and add, 'My parents themselves had a very tight relationship. I felt excluded, and our big house offered me plenty of places to withdraw and hide.'

She found this feeling of exclusion from my parent's relationship interesting and suggests that because they gave Grant away, they didn't have much left for me. Mum's unconscious guilt, as well as looking after her mother and aunt, meant she didn't have much left in the tank. Kari described it 'Like a no-fault divorce, this is a no-fault inherited trauma. It wasn't about you. Any child born in this family and in your birth order would have experienced a similar upbringing.'

If I accept the science presented, then I'm a step closer to accepting that the attachment bond between my mum and me was fractured even before I was born.

Looking at myself in the corner of the screen, I notice I haven't stopped nodding.

Kari believes that I wouldn't have absorbed so much of Dad's pain, sorrow and exclusion, if I'd gotten more from Mum. I would have made different choices and been more solid and less needy. I was set up to feel the loss and grief belonging to my dad, not me, because

I'd lost the connection with Mum. When our core is fractured, it amplifies the feeling of being rejected and alone. Not only was this my life experience summed up in one phrase, it was the dimension of my identity that I consistently hid from the world.

~

It's 6:55 pm. The two-and-a-half-hour session with Kari this morning was enlightening, and I'm still transcribing the notes I scribbled as she was talking. Glancing at the bookshelf, I see 'You're Not Broken'. I wonder what Dr Sarah Woodhouse says about this.

If a child is emotionally neglected, and the parent isn't emotionally in tune with them, things don't go so well. They develop an insecure attachment bond. They may develop a fragmented sense of self, meaning they have a weak identity, and are unclear about who they are, particularly in relationships with others. We call it attachment trauma, but really, it's no different to any other trauma. (page 51)

This was the problem that I had not fully recognised was the problem. I knew the research in epigenetics and had come to understand it was possible that part of the grief I was feeling was not my own. However, after decades of thinking my life was normal, I questioned the validity of naming my experience 'trauma', because I grew up with it being masked and hidden. Sarah named it covert trauma because it's unseen, unknown, and never validated. We ask ourselves, as do others; *did it really happen?*

CHAPTER 29

Honouring

It's November 2022. I see a mature woman walking my way with a wide grin of recognition, her once distinctive ginger hair faded by the insistence of emerging grey. It's Janette. We met in prep and spent thirteen years of education in the same schools. Our mothers were friends and here we are meeting outside St Agnes, the church where they were eager worshippers. I've been sitting in the car, situating myself in last century, scanning the scene, allowing mind pictures to float in and out and wondering who I'll know here today. This is the church opposite Ponsonby, the house of my childhood, built by Great Grandmother Flora, where she, then Kitty, Daphne and Dad all died. It's the house where Grant didn't get to live his life. Janette is the only person from the past who I've spoken with since I found Dad's old leather valise hidden in the Ponsonby attic.

~

6:50 pm on 16 November 2021, my phone pings a Messenger notification with just five words.

'So ... TEDx ... Is it time?'

Feeling my heartbeat pounding, I jump out of the chair and do a couple of laps of the house, trying to think. Is it time? Why not? I've been enthusiastically sharing my detective work and the role generational trauma plays in maintaining secrets. The best part is I feel lighter and brighter. A curtain has been pulled back and, in the mirror's reflection, I see a confident, articulate and validated version of myself that I'm happy for the world (and clients) to see and hear.

My reply: 'It's getting very close …' Send.

'Okay, I'm happy to connect you. Training starts in January, so your talk won't be till February (2022).'

'Okay.' Send.

By 9.00 pm, I'm booked in and preparation begins.

~

'*Do We Need an Identity Label in Order to be Validated?*'

A TEDx Talk under my name is published on YouTube exactly four weeks and four days later for the world to view! Watching the recording for the first time is momentous. Is that really me telling the world:

I'm not a mother.

I'm not a partner or soul mate.

I'm no longer a daughter.

I'm not a sister.

I'm not a widow or divorced.

I'm not a next of kin.

I'll never be a grandmother.

Who am I then?

Where did the calm confidence and composure come from to reveal everything I was not? Details I've kept hidden from my professional world and most of my private connections. It feels like a personal renaissance.

~

A few months later an email landed.

March 2022

Hi Michelle,

Janette ▮▮▮ here. Hope this email finds you well and involved with the things that matter most to you.

I was very moved by your TEDx Talk and its content, knowing you from

St Agnes, Caulfield South State School, and Shelford. I also identified with not being able to label myself the way that others do (i.e. not married, not divorced, not a mother, so not a grandmother, etc. etc.). Three of my grandparents died the year I was born, and I was born after my mum had two miscarriages in close succession. When I was about two, Dad had a nervous breakdown due to war service and time as a prisoner of war in Germany, and Mum was pretty much focused on him and my baby sister.

Just a few years ago, I found out that many of our fellow pupils from Primary School were of Jewish background. From Shelford, of course, we all knew Paulette ███ was Jewish, but Peta ██████████ had always thought her father was Roman Catholic, only to find out after he died that he was actually Jewish and had lost family in the Holocaust. Her daughter ██████ ended up converting to Judaism when she met and married a Jewish boy.

So, life is strange indeed. I knew you had a brother, but not sure when I was aware of it. Mum had said something once, I think when we were talking about the son of my sister's friend being in care because of Down Syndrome, as the family had not been able to cope. I think it was often the norm back then, to put children in care, sad as it seems. I know your mum must've talked about it to some people, because Mum was aware of it, and was also aware of the difficult times your dad had experienced as a German immigrant. I don't know that she knew of his Jewish background. I always remember your mum as a striking woman, very strong and confident, at least from my perspective. I only vaguely remember your dad as a quieter person.

I have time to spend on my hobby of family history and have found many family stories that I never knew about from Mum and Dad and their ancestors and relatives. In recent times, I have photographed many of the plaques in St Agnes Memorial Garden and put them up on findagrave.com.

I find it interesting to look up the names of all the people I remember from my childhood at St Agnes and discover the interconnections from marriages that I never knew of. And, of course, why your home was called Ponsonby!

If you ever want a change from the coaching work you do, you would be a great End of Life Coach (making sense of one's story as one gets older).

Best regards, Janette

~

St Agnes Church Memorial Garden was established for parishioners to inter the ashes of loved ones. The tiny plots are marked with a plaque, and we're here to attend a reunion and service for these families. The pre-TEDx version of myself wouldn't have attended this event, but today I can take the past on. Janette and I find a seat in a packed house. The last official service I attended here was my mother's funeral. The hard wooden pews have been updated with equally hard chairs and there's a refrigerator on the back wall, but everything else looks familiar. Waiting for the service to get underway, my line of vision picks up the stained glass window high to the left, above the altar. I know that the plaque says:

To the Glory of God. The extension of Sanctuary together with the windows and Opus Sectile Mosaic were erected in loving memory of the late Flora Louise Ponsonby Thompson. With the Lord.

The service begins. We stand as one and I'm wondering if Flora commissioned this before her death or was honoured posthumously. If so, by whom? This history distracts me for the next hour.

The last prayers are delivered, the organising team are stacking chairs to clear space for the 'tea party' reunion and folks are milling. I excuse myself and slip out the side door into the garden to have a silent and precious moment with my ancestors. I know exactly where to find them. The brass plaques are attached to the wall, left of the door, in a vertical line. I witnessed the interment of each. My grandparents, John and Kitty, are both present. Mum had kept their ashes in an urn for decades until the Memorial Garden was ready. Below, next in line, is my aunt, Mum's sister Ormee, then her husband Jack. Going up the wall is my dad, his plaque the simplest, bearing his 'Australianised' name Carl Henry, having come here as Karl Heinz. Then my mother. At the top of this line of my family tree is the most recent addition, Grant Phillip.

Bringing his ashes back to Melbourne and back to our parents was the only option I had to complete the circle and honour Grant. It took two years, but he's here. Reading down the wall, I see three generations of my immediate maternal family line are complete. Flora and Daphne are in the Brighton cemetery, but the question still remains. Where are Martha, William and Reuben?

The garden is overgrown now, and the space cramped, so I'm pleased I chose this time before other's relatives emerge and crowd my space. Taking a seat on the old garden bench and leaning on the rusty wrought iron arm, I gaze at the names and try to resurrect the sound of their voices, facial expressions and mannerisms. I wonder how many folks inside having forgotten my father by now, will tell me I look like my mother. Noticing compassion has replaced indifference about the old notion of family, I recall hearing Marine Sélénée's delightful French accent of her audiobook teaching her readers that the way to find resolution is to grant every family member belonging by allowing them their rightful place. I didn't know it at the time, but bringing Grant home has done just that. In this garden, at this moment, I feel the warmth of my parents' love as the Swiss cheese holes of my core continue to shrink and heal.

~

It's three weeks since the Reunion and I'm grateful Janette knows her way around databases as she continues to dig around in the history of the residents of Ponsonby. When I updated cousin John on the events at St Agnes and Janette's interest in genealogy, he reminded me of Flora's death notice, noting Martha as deceased. Neither of us could remember ever seeing Flora's death certificate, though. One of the significant moments during my session with Kari Dunlop was her observation of the other men missing from my genogram and I realise that John and I have assumed the father of the mystery children was Wig, the man of ambiguity named in our Great Grandmother Flora's will. As I'm digging around in Mum's old papers again looking for clues, a simple text message arrives from Janette.

'A present for you,' she writes.

I can see it's a photo of a death certificate, but I need to enlarge it to read the name of the deceased. Oh my goodness! It's Flora. She died at home aged seventy-nine, the same age Kitty died and the same age my mum died. Is this one of the patterns Mark Wolynn asks us to look for?

Is this an identification linking these three women through breaks in the attachment between mother and babies?

Skipping down the screen to the section: Issue in order of birth, the names and ages, I read Kitty sixty-one years, Martha deceased, William fifty-five years, Reuben fifty-three years, Daphne forty-six years.

'I need a calculator to make sense of this,' I message back.

Janette is already on to it, and together we calculate that William was born the same year Flora's husband, my great grandfather John Thompson died in Dunedin. Therefore, Reuben and Daphne must have been born to a different father.

This is a piece of the puzzle I hadn't known I'd been searching for, and there's only one way to join these parts of the family story. Flora returned to Australia, bringing my grandmother Kitty, aged twelve, with her. William aged six and Reuben four did not cross the Tasman, so we assume they were left behind. Janette is now into a New Zealand database and sends me yet another bombshell. Flora remarried the same year my great grandfather died. It seems husband number two, also named John, was Reuben's father. It's confusing, but Janette doesn't seem fazed and continues to mine the resources at her disposal. There is no evidence of the second husband in Australia, but rather John number two spent time in jail before dying seven years later. However, Janette has now discovered proof that both William and Reuben went on to live regular lives in New Zealand. Their identities were kept secret from us and never included in the family narrative.

Time to persist with Mum's diary and letters again, amazed that this was all under my nose for years, but I hadn't uncovered it. Did she know the truth of the boys left behind? Finding a letter written in 1962 from Equity Trustees regarding Flora's estate, my mother was informed of their existence. The upshot is I now know there were two other little boys excluded from the family network, left behind in another country without their mother. Had my mother inherited a predisposition to secrecy too?

Mum knew Daphne must have been born in Melbourne and could not have been Kitty's full sister. Who was Daphne's father? Kari Dunlop was right. There were three boys and two fathers left unseen, unnamed and therefore unacknowledged from my family system. It's like they never existed. Kari had explained that many of us become 'entangled' with the unhappiness of those who came before us, unconsciously adopting destructive familial patterns of anxiety, depression, failure, and even illness in an attempt to 'redo' the past and 'fix' our families. Has this been the energy driving me to find men who were unavailable, didn't want children? Was this my way of ensuring I repeated the pattern of the past?

CHAPTER 30

Destiny

It's May 2021. 'Avuncular', that's it. Mark Wolynn's manner and tone are best described as avuncular. Saying it aloud to no one but myself prompts a memory of Chris, his love of language and the eagerness he had for using a pet word. He'd be proud of my application. I know I can't change the past, but I can wish and my wish for the past is that this framework for identifying inherited family trauma had been available to Chris. Would cancer still have taken him? I will never know, but I'm sure it could have helped him resolve the cause of his Crohn's disease and depression.

I'm watching Class Four of Mark's *Inherited Family Trauma Training* online. Reading his work has been liberating and the session with Kari Dunlop enlightening, so when she offered the opportunity to learn directly from Mark himself, I didn't hesitate. I grabbed it with outstretched arms, not unlike Dr Tronick's baby yearning to regain mum's focus. There are all manner of therapists, counsellors, psychologists, hypnotherapists and coaches in the cohort from around the globe, although I haven't heard another Australian accent yet. There are trauma specialists, family constellation practitioners and a former lawyer writing a book for the American Bar Association about trauma in the legal system. They each have a specialty. For example, Kari's is neuroplasticity. Mark's work is a brand new field very much in the zeitgeist, and this training is designed to add tools to our practitioner's toolbox rather than a workshop for healing our deepest wounds. He acknowledges we're all bringing something of our own story with us.

First week, we looked at the science and the new research. Following on, in the next two segments, Mark revisited the idea of the four unconscious themes foundational to our work. He reminds us we're looking for a break in the early bond with mother, a parent rejected, a merge with a parent or identification with someone in the family other than the parent. The homework from last session are the same as those I'd first used from Mark Wolynn's website where he makes them available to anyone who is curious about their own circumstances. Mark is emphasising the point that the break in the bond doesn't have to be with us. As I learnt, we can inherit it, as we see in the most replicated study in epigenetics, where baby mice were separated from their mothers, and the depressive behaviour showed up for the following three generations. To clarify, Mark adds, we can inherit our mother's broken relationship with her mother, our father's broken relationship with his mother, and we can have our own broken relationship.

After this recap of our last class, Mark illustrates how he works, by breaking down his intake process for a new client. It replicates my experience with Kari last month, and is a mixture of fact finding, teaching and healing. It's a simple concept to accept that, whether it be a physical or mental health issue, it didn't start with us. Yet the number of times over decades, when I have sat in front of various counsellors or doctors, not one has ever asked about what kind of life my parents or great grandparents had. Sarah was the exception.

The next step is a set of written exercises to help us decide what to work on when an individual is seeking help. I recognise these from the preparation Kari sent in readiness for our session. Mark's using an anonymous client case to demonstrate where we begin to investigate the core complaint or problem, be it a health, work or relationship issue they want to focus on and heal. The questions prompt the person to think about something that feels overwhelming, maybe a symptom or a feeling they've had all their life. He suggests a list of possible situations from the hundreds of cases he's worked with, from repeated panic attacks to a fear of flying to Gretchen who, despite trying antidepressants and group therapy, had lived with depression and anxiety for so long that she no longer wanted to live. Mark pauses to acknowledge the gravity of Gretchen's case and his wise eyes look directly into the lens as he says, 'Listen very carefully to the impact of any emotionally charged language and particular words the client is using to describe their worries and struggles. They can say more than you realise.'

This signals that we're moving into the part of the training where Mark teaches his Core Language Map, the blueprint for all our detective work. When the assistants were introduced earlier, Anna, who has worked with Mark for years and has a background in clinical hypnotherapy and integrated body psychotherapy, said 'the core language approach has helped me so much in just getting to the root cause right from that first session'. We don't need complex questionnaires or fancy psychometric tests, we just need to ask and listen. What if I added some of these questions into the pre-program reflective journalling, I ask my new clients to do? Will it help me get to the heart of their identity stories?

Listening to and watching Mark deliver a case study brings tangible meaning to his theory. We're hearing about Joanne, who wants to find 'the one' who can give her what she missed in childhood. She wants 'someone who understands me, sees me and has lots of energy'. Joanne either chooses men who aren't passionate enough, men who won't commit to her or men who had terrible traumas. Her mother wasn't emotional, she was always depressed and so she says, 'I spent my childhood trying to connect with her but could never reach her emotionally.' Then Mark gives us the mother's story, which included her father dying when she was two. Grandmother found a new husband and gave mother to her father's parents to raise. This broken attachment would have shrunk the mum's emotional repertoire, dialling her back emotionally and leaving her with a limited capacity to give to her own child, Joanne. As a child, Joanne had to pull her own energy in so she wouldn't push her mother away. When she feels a man is shut down or becomes too quiet, she becomes aggressive with him. When she chooses men who won't commit to her or men who have had terrible traumas or difficult lives themselves, she repeats her early relationship with her mother, reliving the emotional disconnect of the trauma of her mother.

This case study has given the theory colour and energy. All the clues were in Joanne's complaints, descriptions of her mother and the dynamics of her childhood. We didn't need a leather couch, pipe and certificates to see what's happening. I'm thinking about all my past relationships right now and would relish an opportunity to meet Joanne and compare notes. Mum used to say, 'I never had that maternal bone inside me.' Mark Wolynn would say she didn't receive enough love to then give maternally.

~

Just as summer 2022 begins the transition to autumn, garden colours appear more muted after months of harsh, blazing sun. The leaves haven't turned yet, but they look exhausted. Today is a fresh reprieve after yesterday's steamy humidity and I take a moment to settle myself. The soothing water song floats up from the creek, and parrots, lorikeets and kookaburras watch over me. I'm still intrigued by Mark Wolynn's Core Language Map and the journalling suggestions he so generously shares in his book. Sarah has been the guiding star, budging me to examine the past and unlock the secrets, and Mark is a remote conductor dropping in the next stanza. It's a progression from dark to light, from heavy to bright.

I've been writing in my journal as instructed, following the order of the exercises before reading on to the next chapter. At times, I've felt resistant and, yes, I've been avoiding the next tough stage. Today is the day to excavate and refine *Written Exercise #6: Identifying Your Core Sentence*. I have to tackle the exhausting nagging hollowness again, hoping it will unlock a final door, and I reread where I finished my first attempt.

The worst thing that could happen to me is I will die alone. If this state continues, I will be forgotten, will have left no legacy and it will be the end of the Scheibner story. It won't be long before no one remembers me.

That's more than one sentence though. Mark insists we need to keep digging until we flush out the hidden underlying fear and anxieties that he believes originate within us. It could be an inherited fear or an early childhood trauma. We know we have it when it's brief and contains dramatic, emotionally charged language and creates a physical reaction in our body when spoken. I don't think I've found it yet. If I'm going to do this properly, I need to persist. Here I go. Writing down where I left off last time, *The worst thing that could happen to me is I will die alone.* This time I add, *just like Grant did, and just like my grandparents, separated in a death camp, and forgotten.*

Reading the statement slowly, I give my heart time to catch up to my mind,

And *if that happened, then what? what would be the worst part of that?*

Eyes closed, listening, waiting, the pen takes over.

When I die, it will be like I never existed!

Looking down, the page is blurred. I can't make out the last word. My shoulders lift with tension, my core clenched tighter than a drum, eyes close again as tears burn down my face and I realise I'm not breathing. I've found it.

~

Mark is recapping and wrapping up this week's class. He's reminding us that we're not born with a clean hard drive but rather an operating system that has the content of the emotional residue of the traumas of our family. I'm seeing this and the other trainings I've completed since Chris passed away, in addition to all the books I've been reading and all the conversations I've been having with Sarah, as part of a greater solution. And an alternative version of my story is emerging. Sometimes, the simple act of linking our experience to an unresolved trauma in our family is enough.

Then, tuning back into the closing remarks, I hear 'you cannot truly heal until you let go of the story'. But if I let go of the story, what's left? Who am I without the story? On the one hand, my life was normal. Mum and I were close. On the other hand, the story explains why I've failed to meet social and personal expectations. I'm feeling resistant again. *Let go of the story. Let go of the story. Let go of the story!* Hang on, Mish, remember Old McDonald's Farm? You learnt the story was just a bunch of words. And what did you learn from Judith Glaser? *Change your words to change the world.* And what did you learn from Dr David Drake? *It's not the story itself that's important, it's how it makes you feel.*

The screen is blank. Avuncular Mark is finished for this week. I open the journal and look at the page where I've written my single short core sentence.

When I die, it will be like I never existed!

Reading it again, my heart is again pounding, not with shock, but with recognition. It's so familiar to me, yet I had never before consciously formed this sentence in my head, and certainly had never spoken the words. For years, I've been complaining of never being seen or heard within the family. In a journal entry dated early 2016, I'd written,

I'm going to die without ever having had someone look at me like I'm their world.

On many occasions in my life, when relationships were crippling or finishing, when the loneliness was simply too much and the ingrained feelings of grief were exhausting, when I couldn't see a way out of my current mire, I'd go to bed and, in the dark, I would plan my escape. Where could I go? Different options would come up, and it wasn't to end my life. It was to disappear and have no further contact with anyone ever again. When I was feeling so alone and disconnected, I'd go back to this strategy: first rule, don't tell a soul; second, send money away slowly in advance then move it again; third, go as far as possible so I can *never* be found. My secret strategy, my plan B for as long as I can recall, has been to exclude myself and never be found.

Now captured in one new single sentence is the core fear that has driven my lived experience. Evidence that this is not just part of my story, but it's my identity. Biological and emotional inheritance may be our reality, but it doesn't have to be our destiny.

I think this solution is going to lead me to a more accepting self.

CHAPTER 31

Traces

It's the first day of January 2023. I'm not one for New Year's resolutions. I prefer to land a word as a guide for my intention in the coming year. Opening my A3 sketchpad, I write *ILLUMINATION* across the top of a fresh page. Before I get going, it's time to flick back to 2022 and finish my reflections on the year in review. Last January, I'd hoped for *EXPANSION*, and although my business hadn't grown, my mind, heart and self-identity have deepened and settled in a place of expanded possibility. The version of a Venn diagram, sketched during a chat with Karyn, a trusted friend and business colleague, sits centre page. I remember the day vividly. We were sharing notes on favourite podcasts, and I added, 'You'd love *Family Secrets*! Dani Shapiro has written four memoirs, including *"Inheritance"* in which she reveals her own family secret.'

'Every family has a secret, so who wouldn't be interested?' said Karyn.

'Indeed, I listened to a bonus episode where Dani interviewed Dr Galit Atlas, an award-winning psychoanalyst who's published her book *'Emotional Inheritance'*. I can't wait to read that, too.'

'Is it a memoir?' Karyn asks.

'No, although she does include her own inherited trauma secrets intertwined with her patients' stories and research. Dani asked Galit about why she wrote the book, and listen to this, she said this helps us identify the links between our life struggles and the "emotional inheritance" we all carry'.

Karyn is on to this quickly and adds, 'I know what it feels like. How often have we talked about this?'

'Yep, Galit says that it's only by following the traces that ghosts leave that we can change our destiny!'

As I listened to the new spirit in my voice, I saw an image of a heart with a cloud overlapping its lower third and a tear drop intersecting with both. In the centre space where all three met, I saw the words *My Identity*. It reminded me of the many times I've heard Dani Shapiro say, 'I've become a student of secrets.' During 2022, I realised I'd become a student of identity.

~

'Do you have children?'

It's 2016 and I'm tired, troubled and suited up as Professional Michelle. I've lost count of how often this question trips me up. Now it hangs in the air above the table like a balloon filled with water. It swells, getting bigger and bigger, and I know if it bursts it will be messy. A grief counsellor I was seeing after Mum died suggested I have a prepared answer in the form of a practiced response, like a safe phrase for these exact situations. In this moment, though, the question ties my tongue in a knot yet again, just like it always does, every Mother's Day, and with every new person I meet. I can feel my smile slowly fading into a blank stare. My jaw is locking, teeth clenching, voice evaporating. I simply can't remember my safe phrase, such is the power of this question. Why does it always shut me down?

Sitting in the cramped meeting room, with glass walls open to the passing world, Carla, a potential coaching client, sits opposite. This is a meet and greet for her to decide if I'm the right fit, and I can't speak. After a very long, uncomfortable pause, I manage to croak, 'Why do you ask?'

'Because as a mother ...'

Aha! I catch myself thinking, before she's even finished the sentence. *And, there it is! Right there! Identity Label: 'Mother'.*

Inside that label, there is a complex web of assumption and permission to which I feel I have no right. I sit in this awkward silence, something I have learnt to excel in, and my mind is an echo chamber repeating, *No I don't have kids. Please don't judge me. I'm still a good person. I'm excellent at my job.* I want to say, *You're meeting me as an executive coach. Why are you asking me if I have kids? Why aren't you asking me about my credentials and experience?*

Carla is still speaking '... because as a working mother, I think it's important that my coach be a mother, too.'

At the risk of losing a needed work opportunity, I ignore the question and her answer and explain my perspective on how I would approach her leadership development needs based on the briefing the sponsoring manager provided. I propose a strategy to focus on strengthening her leadership brand and using those attributes to build influence and presence as a leader. But it's still awkward, and I leave the meeting feeling ashamed, sad, and mute.

On the drive back, I try to reset myself before I get back to Chris. Today's meeting was scheduled to fit around his chemo appointments, and I don't want to take this home with me. Pulling over, I leave the engine running, close my eyes and try to breathe from the diaphragm. I see an image slowly form. It's an endless waterfall of tears coming from another place in time. *Where is this coming from? Why do I react so quickly and sadly?* Then I begin to hear those words on a repeating loop yet again, *just bringing myself through my past into the present has been exhausting. Why has fate conspired to have me do it alone? Why?*

~

First mission on the *Illumination* calendar is to read *Emotional Inheritance.* I deliberately haven't made any plans for the next week so I can crack through it. It's been enlightening to discover fellow pilgrims finding resolution and sharing their research and experience with me—okay, with the world—but it feels like it's directed at me. When Galit Atlas said she's always curious to understand her patients' life choices, why they choose to have or not have relationships, family or career, her words sing to me. Why hadn't I reached my full potential? It's validating as it all comes together. I want to master this. Dealing with secrets could be the key I need to turn. Understanding how we secretly inherit elements of the unspoken lives of relatives who went before us and how their contribution impacts our identity, even now, feels like I'm on the cusp of repairing another layer. I continue to move from Swiss cheese to vintage Cheddar.

Galit Atlas says we need our torches to illuminate everything that we leave down in the basement of life, everything that prevents us from moving forward, living and truly loving. I metaphorically high five her. Galit Atlas thinks it will help us find our life purpose and allow us to move forward. I'm absolutely convinced that I've been on the right path, joining dots and finding themes, rather than seeing the past as a shadowy vault of trouble. I wonder if we learn more about these hidden origins and reconcile with the past, will we then discover our special X factor? Is this the magic formula of self-identity?

There are so many highlights in *'Emotional Inheritance'*. How can I remember them for my next chat with Karyn? The patient case studies include third generation survivors, forbidden love, infidelity, loss of a sibling, conflicted motherhood choices, physical abuse, friendship and painful loss. Eager to stay in the moment with the author, I use the phone audio to record talking points to send to Karyn later.

- Do the memories of those who raised us live on inside us?
- How do we inherit, hold and process things that we don't remember or didn't experience ourselves?
- Do we want to move forward but get caught in the same cycle over and over?
- Find the first childhood memory. It often conceals within it the main ingredients of future therapy.
- Everything we don't consciously know about ourselves has the power to control and run our lives. Does it matter that we don't know, assuming our ancestor's trauma finds its way into our minds, anyway?
- Why do so many people want love or a career but can't find it?

Galit Atlas was also raised with silence being used as a tool to erase unpleasant events and memories and her insights prompt me to ask questions of myself.

- Grant was officially my parents' firstborn. Did Dad's traumatic past live in Grant's body?

- How far does being loyal to family myths and legacies go? Maybe Mum didn't tell me about Grant when I was engaged to Matthew because she was protecting me from having a Down Syndrome child. Was it her fear before it was mine?
- What if I'd had a Downs baby and repeated my parents' decision? Was this their deeply hidden regret? Their shame? Could I have coped with a limited ability child? Their fear or mine?
- What are my untold family stories that have been re-enacted over and over?
- Why did I decide to have this tattoo on my arm? Was it to honour Chris or was it a covert nod to Elly and Ludwig? Did they have numbers tattooed on their arms? Did their families honour their memory?

I love my A3 sketchpad. Every page is dated so I can track the development of my ideas. The *Iceberg* image created three years before is now gifting me newfound meaning and has morphed into a model for *Identity*. At the base is DNA, members of the family system, (the source of secrets), because cracking the secrets has been the doorway to my understanding of what's passed forward. I'm calling it an identity inheritance.

Everything we don't consciously know about ourselves has the power to control and run our lives in the same way the riptides below the surface of the ocean are its most powerful forces. ('Emotional Inheritance', p87)

What are the secrets I've kept from myself? Wow, this is thought provoking. Time for a session with Sarah. Why did fate deprive me of children? Was it loyalty? Fear? Identification with Grant? A defence mechanism all layered upon three inherited generations with breaks in the bond between mothers and their babies?

~

Sarah's smile lights up the screen as always. Back when she asked if I was ready to finish therapy with her or continue, I purposefully elected to continue. Sarah has been holding the light high up over the path to illuminate my way from one stepping stone to the next since 2016. It's all very well to understand the theories, but exploring and interpreting through conversation is truly transformational. There have been many times when she's had to remind me how far I've come in understanding the impact of decisions taken by my ancestors. Now I can see how my own choices have been protecting me.

'Sarah, I've found another book, *"Emotional Inheritance"*. You probably know the author, Galit Atlas?'

She nods, so I keep going, such is my drive to understand.

'One of the case studies is the story of Rachel who goes to see Galit to discuss her ambivalence about having children. Her conscious reasons are not my conscious reasons, so I wasn't sure if there was anything in this chapter for me, until Rachel says that she's always wanted to live in Israel.'

I'm on a roll and Sarah, as always, allows me the space to get it out.

'This is crazy, but the unexplained pull to visit Israel has never gone away for me, either. Rachel is Jewish, I'm not. Yet despite knowing so little of my Jewish heritage, I feel it. It's a trace in my blood. It's part of who I am.'

'Michelle, you've spoken of absorbing your dad's survivor mindset, especially with money. It runs much deeper than that. Remembering and re-enacting suffering is part of the Jewish tradition. Rituals like the Passover Seder are stories of redemption from slavery in ancient Egypt and have shaped Jewish consciousness, values and identity. But for your dad and his parents, the celebrations of survival would have taken place in hiding, reinforcing the secret for him.'

'Would being Jewish have been part of Dad's identity then, even though they baptised him so young?'

'Yes, his mother Elly was Jewish and Judaism is passed down through the mother,' Sarah reminds me.

'I can't begin to imagine what it was like for him, with Mum such a committed Anglican. Not only did he lose his family, he must have felt the loss that those faith rituals provide in challenging times.'

Reading Rachel's case reminds me of how we learn when we see ourselves reflected in the stories of others. Rachel wished she knew more, but her family story was silenced, too. She says as a little girl she was afraid of everything, as was I. I've told Sarah before how I was terrified of dogs for no apparent reason. I still have a very low tolerance for sudden loud noise. I screamed having childhood vaccinations, and I refused to go to the doctor. I still have a panic response in the dentist's chair. I was a child who couldn't sleep without the hall light on, so afraid of the dark I was, and I still like a night light on somewhere in the house. And vomiting still sends me into an extreme panic.

Rachel's childhood memories are much clearer than mine. She says she couldn't tell anyone about her fears and as she talks about them, she realises she couldn't bear the idea of having a baby, assuming they would experience life the way she did. Did I FEAR having a baby?

'Galit asks Rachel what her grandfather's secret was, and Rachel whispers, "Who knows?" Wow, unconscious impact!'

Not long after that session, Rachel brings her baby girl to see Galit. Naming her fear provided a clearing for her to have a child. When night tremors return, she continues to engage in psychotherapy to fully understand the layers of past generational loss. I wonder if I'd had the benefit of research into epigenetics and the knowledge of generational trauma when I was in my twenties and thirties, would I have had a child?

Despite the unexplained fears, I'm robust and resilient. I've survived the emotional pain of deep and repeated loss. Sarah and I remark simultaneously that I've also inherited the capacity, courage and strength of my Jewish family line to just keep going.

CHAPTER 32

Healing

It's August 2023.

'You're different, Michelle! I've known you over twenty years, but I've never seen you so lit up and content.'

I met Diane on the first day of the Landmark Forum two decades ago. She did the Old McDonald's Farm task with me. We went on to do a number of personal development programs together, residential affairs with very long days. Billionaire Bootcamp, Presentation and Platform Skills, Design Your Destiny ... We know the other well. But Diane moved to the Gold Coast, Chris was ill, then we were locked down and whilst we've spoken by phone, we haven't been in each other's company. She knows my life complaints and I know hers. This weekend, we've been walking and talking and several times she's commented on the new version of me she's experiencing.

'You have a lighter, more joyful energy now,' Diane adds.

The moment I hear her words, I recognise how far I've come. I love Diane's curiosity and value her thoughts. We continually exchange new wisdoms we've picked up and she introduced me to the new Oprah Winfrey podcast launched around the time her book, 'What Happened to You?' was published.

'How do you mean?' I ask.

'I know we've spoken on the phone, but I haven't been in your presence for years and there's definitely a transformed energy about you that I haven't felt before.'

'Transformed energy, meaning?' I know I'm probing, but it's so interesting and I can rely on Diane for honest advice.

'You had a heavier energy before. You're not as worried now. You seem happier. Do you feel different?' Diane asks as we head out for a last walk before she heads off.

'I do, yes! Thank you for noticing. I'd describe it as a more focused energy.'

'You've always been motivated with your work, but now it's like you've found your true purpose and you're going about it in a more intentional and soulful way,' Diane observes.

'Yes, that is totally what I hope I'm doing. It doesn't mean there aren't times when I slip back, but I recognise what's happening now and I can regulate my response and recalibrate quickly.'

We've walked down on to the beach and continue to talk as we head to a coffee stop.

Diane asks, 'I know you've read a lot and really absorbed the research, so how have you integrated it all into your body?'

Diane has been mediating, using intention setting, goals and affirmations for many years, so it's an interesting and informed question.

'I describe it now as finding my self-identity. Remember when Chris passed, and I was so bogged down in what I didn't have that I lost sight of who I was? Week after month after year, Sarah metaphorically held my hand and urged me to consider and uncover new perspectives. I'd walk through her door and be wrapped in an invisible cloak of safety so I could face the past and unpack the trials of my parents and their parents without judgement. Each session was a time-bound capsule of support and then I'd drive home feeling heard.'

The wind is strong, blowing us backwards almost, and making it hard to hear. We're both content to just walk and think. We can pick this up over coffee. It has me thinking about phases of change and transformation, though. What did I need to leave behind in order to move toward something new?

Sitting in the Winey Cow (everyone loves the name), Diane asks, 'If you were a guest on a podcast and the interviewer asked something like *I want what you're having,* what would be your five top tips?'

'Wow, now you have me thinking! First, I'd say, have a look inside the invisible backpack you carry with you every day and see what's weighing you down. Be curious, pick up your journal and see what you uncover. Name the complaints, problems or symptoms in there. Then become a detective. What stories didn't get told? What secrets were tightly held? Label the signposts. Next, try to read beneath the story you're telling yourself. Note how it makes you feel. You must be willing to let go of the story to create space for a new narrative to unfold.'

I hear myself echoing an amalgam of everything I've uncovered from reading my books and listening to experts over the past six years.

~

The question of how to share my learnings with others stayed with me after Diane left. Thinking about using metaphors to create pivots for clients reminded me of my sketchbook. I'd be lost without my 120-page spiral bound 110gsm A3 companion. It's heavy and the pages are becoming dog-eared, but it's captured the path I've taken to get to the other side. Flicking through the date pages, all the topics I played with are there. I can see the tables, flowcharts and brace maps where I've captured the theories and frameworks from the experts and interpreted meaningful applications to my situation. I see these as blueprints. But I also see the development of thinking captured in various mind maps, bubble diagrams, brainstorming messes, including my own version of heart, mind and body where I now believe self-identity resides.

~

April 2021, Kari Dunlop has collected the contents from my virtual backpack, we've made the links and it's time for resolution.

'Now we're going to do an eyes-closed contemplation with some of your family and then a longer piece with your mum and lastly a longer piece with you.'

As she continues, I hear the tone of resistance in my reply, 'Are you saying, then, that the main issue for me has been the lack of attachment with Mum? Because I thought that the exhaustion and the sadness and the loneliness and the ah, what's the word ... that, you know, that lack of tomorrow's-going-to-be-good kind of attitude came from my dad. You know, when I think about what's been the most overwhelming and present emotion in my life, it's the feeling of being heartbreakingly alone. Now I know it belonged to Dad not me. He experienced post-traumatic stress, both from his experience in Germany and then his experience in the internment camp. He learnt to silence and suppress his Jewishness from his mum. And I really feel the burden of that,' I blurt out without even taking a breath, almost crying again.

Kari nods and patiently continues the educating section, repeating what I've read, but knowing I need to hear it again in a slightly different way.

'Yes, because that's what we remember. But that comes later. It's the earlier trauma that we don't remember that lives in our body, in our nervous system. This lays the foundation. It's almost like we're set up for loss and feeling sad and grieving because of that loss of connection from mum, and you would have inherited it from your dad's break with his mum and then your mum's break with her mum. You got the trifecta. On top of that is the stuff that happened when you were younger. That's what we can cognitively make connections out of. But we can't remember what went before because we were babies. I think just understanding that it happened earlier can be beneficial. Later, when we feel this aloneness, it's what we felt as a baby. If we had gotten more from mum, we wouldn't have felt so bad growing up.'

I'd been protecting Mum's memory, and trying to stay loyal to her decisions. In seeing the connections to the past and accepting that it didn't start with her, either, feels like a huge breakthrough. I can now go into the eyes closed process with an open heart. First step is for me to imagine welcoming Grant, then Elly and Ludwig and then anyone else who was excluded and never talked about, into my mind.

Kari is speaking the words for me, acknowledging the reasons they were unable to leave a legacy. 'With your inside voice, tell Elly and Grant, "I, too, feel like I'll die alone, and I've had this feeling and this fear for so long. I feel like I, too, will have no legacy as if I'd never existed. I now know these aren't my feelings. My fears didn't start with me, and I know this isn't what you want for me. These feelings started with you." Now invite your father in. Picture them all standing at your back, supporting you to succeed. Hear them say to you, "We stand behind you, supporting you, loving you, blessing you to live a full vibrant connected life. From now on when you feel those tears come up, the sadness, the grief, remember us standing behind you. Even light a candle for each of us. Feel us blessing you, knowing that you are the spearhead. Everything that we hope for is for you to live our hopes and our dreams and our wishes. When you do well, we do well, even in the spirit world. If your life goes well, everything is worth it. All the ways we suffered, nothing is wasted.

Take a few breaths in as they offer a blessing. *"We're smiling on you."*

This is truly awesome. Sitting quietly, eyes still closed, I see the burden falling away as a light breeze takes it off into the sunset. I'm now one hundred per cent ready as I move into the next phase with Mum. The resistance in my body is still there, but I can silently engage with the process, and trust that with ongoing practice my core will heal.

~

Six months after the session, Sarah and I have continued to reframe my reactions to situations through this historical lens and it feels time for the next steps in honouring their legacy. I know exactly what I want to do. Pulling out old albums, I find the one photo of a smiling Grant where I can see a glimpse of Dad and, yes, I have a perfect size frame for it. Then I find one of Mum, looking beautifully younger than the sad memories of her later years, holding a very young baby me on Christening Day. Now I'm looking for Dad, and I find Elly and Ludwig still living in the frame from my first and only memories of them. I'm looking for Dad as a hopeful young man and here's the perfect photo. His dark brown eyes looking directly at me through the camera lens, and I can see myself reflected in him. My parents go into a frame together and they all come out of the dark and upstairs into the bright warmth of the home where I have found peace. Looking for a place where I can see them every day, speak to them if I wish, place flowers or candles on anniversaries, I settle on a central place where any visitors can acknowledge them, too. Standing back, I feel as light as a feather. This is momentous. It's the first time my birth family has been together in one place.

~

Recently watching a rom com movie, the evergreen question came up. The central woman was asked what she really wanted in a relationship. She replied, a partner who sees only her, a wildly passionate no-choice connection. *I get it,* I said to the screen, *it's still eluding me, too.* As my recovery continues and I design the next phase of life, there is still one thing missing. I've accepted that not having my own children has been the collateral damage of history. Nonetheless, there's still a place of longing in my heart. Many of the phone calls between Diane and me over the years, as far back as the times I was trying to free myself from Matthew, have entailed dissecting the behaviour of men in our fraught liaisons. I make a note to self to share Mark Wolynn's *21 Invisible Dynamics* that can affect relationships with her. I'd forgotten these insights. Rereading now, I see that I'd circled three of the twenty-one still holding meaning for me.

A break in the bond with mother is on the list, and I'm aware of how that plays out now and, although it describes the former version of me, it's no longer a factor. Next point affirms if your parent or grandparent remained alone after, say, the death of a spouse, you might stay alone as well. When Dad died, I was just twenty-three and my mother remained living alone for the next seventeen years. 'As if in silent allegiance, you unconsciously find a way to share the loneliness'—bam, it comes at me from another angle. Thirdly, I identified with an older sibling in the family who didn't marry.

The more self-blame, regret and shame I let go of, especially around the unmarried label, the more self-compassion and life within me is emerging. This crusade has helped me see what I hadn't been able to see because I was blind to what had impacted me. Being received in a multi-dimensional way now is to be truly known, understood, valued and honoured. I've found my authenticated voice.

Epilogue

When death triggered grief, a melancholy hidden so profoundly that I had never named it, rose to the surface. It sent me into a state of mourning I hadn't expected and didn't manage well. It was complicated: I was single, voiceless, childless and I couldn't shake the belief that I was doing this alone, family-less.

'*The childless have no legacy after death, once the memory fades,*' a quote from Sian Prior's second memoir, *Childless*.

The stakes were high. The only part of my identity remaining intact was my professional persona, working in the realm of personal branding, helping clients find their purpose and express it through their authentic selves. Yet, behind that, *Who was I? What would be my legacy?*

Since then, the paths I've travelled have been a crusade, searching for self-understanding and both internal and external validation. I have motored along a freeway, unsure of the destination, reading the overhead signs, taking slip roads, lingering in the service centres. Yet, I continued forward, never turning back. In doing so, I have arrived where I didn't know I needed to go.

Now I have the map.

~

Looking at the map now, I can trace the route I embarked on. The car was fuelled with a deep systemic grief triggered by the death of a significant loved one. I was an adult orphan, with a missing backdrop of yarns, facts, photos and memories. What I had was a gaping absence of story. The first turn off taken was to name the causes triggering the expedition. The car boot was stuffed with family secrets, echoes of generational pain and intergenerational trauma. I was driving unconsciously carrying feelings, symptoms, behaviours and the hardships of others. The backseat driver, an entangled family system with an attachment relationship blueprint that I couldn't see or hear.

It became apparent that if I was to find my way, I must look in the rear-view mirror and adopt the mindset of a detective tracing historical breadcrumbs. In my collection paternal grandparents who were holocaust victims, a father who fled the holocaust but faced persecution by Nazi detainees and suffered a breakdown in an Australian internment camp. My brother, born with Down Syndrome, sent away to an institution shortly after birth, as my mother planned for a replacement baby. Each detail carried unhealed despair of others, so painful it was passed down to the next generation who remain loyal to the decisions of those who went before.

With all of this input in my GPS, I followed directions to meet the invisible impact of the past on my playbook. Unspoken truths, shame and loss maintained by silence led to me attributing meaning to patterns that weren't accurate. Turning off onto the first service road, I was greeted by my own life patterns, where choosing belonging over safety led me to partners as I tried to heal the past but was left voiceless and needy. And with a preference for being alone as a way to alleviate the fear of being abandoned.

During every road trip, it's essential to take breaks. So, I veered off the road, finding solace under trees beside a brook, away from traffic and people. Gazing at the beautiful sky of a late sunrise, I was struck by the realisation that my identity story hadn't begun the day I was born. It was unusually exciting to consider myself multi-faceted in a completely refreshing way. This new energy was the impetuous to explore further. Pausing, beneath the rising sun I read, learnt and investigated. Science confirmed my Jewish blood and research introduced epigenetics into the equation. Learning the four unconscious themes impacting us as result of intergenerational trauma, confirmed the possibility my relationship choices had ensured I did not have a family. What my brother couldn't have I would not have. Unintentionally being single and childless was a feature of my identity, and shame trained me to become very skilled in hiding it, fearing others would judge me as a failure. My brother's legacy of invisibility had become my state of living.

Leaving the quietness of the roadside haven, I resumed the journey. In naming the triggers and causes of who I'd become, I accepted the solutions offered. My pain was genuine, not imagined. Yet, you can't heal trauma in secret, and you must be willing to lose the story in order to diffuse the charge.

It's not what our parents did, it's that we're still holding on to it.

~

With the veil lifted on this persistent search for external endorsements of my value, I could see hiding the truth had become part of who I was. Without the labels the world loads up with meaning, like partner and mother, I had constantly needed validation. This concept resonated deeply, prompting me to address it on the TEDx platform by asking the question: 'Do We Need an Identity Label in Order to be Validated?' Viewers shared their own stories of family secrets, including reasons for those secrets deliberately hidden from them and the secrets they continue to hide from others. In this shared experience, I found solace—I was not alone.

Memoirs by Adam Frankel, Dani Shapiro, and Sian Prior introduced me to a community of professionals who, like myself, had private, invisible secrets cluttering the version of the identities they'd been living with.

Healing has been a multifaceted process. Uncovering and facing the details of my past—who I was, my origins, experiences and my lineage— has connected me to my heritage and deepened my appreciation for those who had gone before, to their choices and decisions. As I pieced together each fragment, I could see my heritage looking back at me, finally soaking into my mind and heart. I found self-identity and self-compassion.

I've emerged stronger, braver and wiser. I am enough.

Acknowledgements and Gratitude

To Sarah Sacks, who witnessed and guided me through grief, discovery and healing.

To Kelly Irving, without whom *Hush* would never have been born.

To her Expert Author Community, including Sarah Martin, Robert Andersson, Melo Calarco, Mark Berridge and Peter Scott for support, accountability and friendship.

To Deb Lee for believing there was an audience for my story and the encouragement to keep going.

To David Brewster for sending me away to read and understand memoir.

To Alison Wearing for teaching the value of memoir as a legacy for reaching the readers I hope to serve.

To Sian Prior for mentoring and fine tuning my writing.

To Natasha Gilmour for feeling my vision and so respectfully bringing *Hush* to your bookshelves.

Heartfelt thanks:

To Chris Milne, who trusted and chose me to walk beside him to the end, gifting me the opportunity of discovering my capacity for unconditional love.

To John Boxshall, who has been quietly in the background since the day I was born.

To Bec Lanham, Michael Sherer and Nikita Brown for their persistence in showing me a new meaning of 'family'.

'Don't urge me to leave you or to turn back from you. Where you go I will go, and where you stay I will stay.' Ruth 1:16

To Kez Viner and Ben Boxshall for our renewed family friendship.

To Phil Andersen, for being my greatest cheerleader, dining companion and outstanding friend.

To April Jarrett for finding Grant and to Janette Agg for filling in the Ponsonby gaps.

To the tribe of women led by Bec who continue to love and listen to me: Karyn Lynch Diane Hocking, Justine Jacono, Betty McGrath, Bev de Kretser, Annalise Jennings, Karen Faehndrich, Viv Granger, and Gloria Lew. Your input and guidance lies between each page.

'Family are the people who fight for you even when you make mistakes.
Remind you of who you are when you forget.
Save you when you need saving.
Give you what you need to save yourself.' Anonymous

If you're still reading, thank you—you are the audience this was written for.

About the Author

Michelle Scheibner

MICHELLE SCHEIBNER is passionate about personal learning and growth, health, fitness, and loves getting on her fruit box to talk about the power of personal brand identity story. Originally drawn to the world of fashion design, her academic path had other ideas and she enrolled in a Bachelor of Arts after completing Year 12. Her tertiary qualifications took her back into school as a teacher and fashion was relegated to a diversion. By the time Michelle stepped away from salaried employee, she had held management and leadership positions in education, consulting and business development, cutting her commercial teeth working in England for three years.

Since establishing her coaching practice in 2004, Michelle has provided services developing and delivering programs including leadership effectiveness, competency frameworks, future leader career management and change strategies to support people through large scale business transformations. She's worked across a range of levels including regional heads, CEOs, directors and senior managers. Michelle has partnered with and mentored many executives to achieve personal high value transitions both in their corporate and entrepreneurial endeavours.

Michelle developed a reputation for working with successful professionals to articulate and amplify their personal brand as a way of generating leadership presence and influence. She also developed a reputation for asking the difficult questions pushing accomplished individuals to recognise their hybrid identity was a gift positioning them for accelerated success and fresh satisfaction. Then she turned the questions on herself.

In 2020, Michelle stepped out from behind the carefully managed professional brand she'd been wearing all her working life. Over three years, she delved into research and introspection, culminating in her memoir, *Hush*. Adding to her postgraduate qualifications in Career Development, Social Branding, and Image Management, alongside studies in Narrative Coaching, Conversational-IQ, she added Inherited Family Trauma. Her true legacy emerged. *Hush* is a case study of events illustrating the intersection of history, culture, beliefs and genetics, shaping Michelle into the coach, mentor, speaker and author she is today.

Michelle's coaching and mentoring practice has grown organically through networks and champions and now advises expert speakers and authors in how to unlock and activate their visibility through unearthing the why, what and how of their stories. They discover their gift for communicating intentionally with the world.

And for Michelle, personal styling remains a relaxing passion driven by intuition. These days she's happy for her fashion choices to stand out in a crowd. She considers style to be an extension of how she wants to feel, accomplish, create and contribute. Colour is an integral feature of Michelle's style and wearing sunset, sunrise tones always brings her joy, confidence and optimism.

~

I'd love you to come back and tell me what has changed for you since reading *Hush*. Have you honoured a loved one? Found your self-identity? Your voice? Your true purpose? Let's explore how the book has impacted you.

michellescheibner.com